Orange Book

Critical Thinking with Literature

Reading • Writing • Communicating

by

Dorothy Kauffman, Ph.D.

University of Maryland

ISBN 0-8454-2454-8

CONTINENTAL PRESS
Elizabethtown, PA 17022

Credits

Cover Design and Art Direction: Kirchoff/Wohlberg, Inc.

Interior Design: Kevin Miller

Illustration: Pages 6, 8–10, 13, 41–43, 54, 76, 78, 99, 111, Ray Burns; Pages 12, 18, 69, 79, 86, 92, 105, Keith Force; Pages 14–16, Liz Callen; Pages 19, 20, 22, 39, 60, 61, 77, 87, 94, 112, V. Carlin Verreaux; Pages 25–28, James Ransome; Pages 32–36, Arieh Zeldich; Pages 49–52, Rosekrans Hoffman; Pages 57–58, Don Madden; Pages 62–65, 70–73, Floyd Cooper; Pages 80–82, Lyle Miller; Pages 88–90, Konrad Hack; Page 94, Kevin Miller; Page 95, Lou Vaccaro; Pages 101–103, Steve Cieslawski; Pages 108–109, Esther Baran

Photography: Page 5, Robert E. Kauffman

Acknowledgments

Every effort has been made to trace the ownership of all copyrighted material and to secure the necessary permissions to reprint these selections. In the event of any question arising as to the use of any material, the editor and the publisher, while expressing regret for any inadvertent error, will be happy to make the necessary correction in future printings. Grateful acknowledgment is made to the following for permission to reprint the copyrighted material listed below:

The Land Where Ice Cream Grows by Anthony Burgess. Copyright © 1979 by Anthony Burgess. Reprinted by permission of Doubleday, a division of Bantam, Doubleday, Dell Publishing Group, Inc.

"I, Icarus" from *Bread, Wine and Salt* by Alden Nowlan. Copyright © 1967 by Irwin Publishing. Reprinted by permission of Stoddart Publishing Co. Limited, 34 Lesmill Rod., Don Mills, Ontario, Canada.

Journey to Jo'burg: A South African Story by Beverley Naidoo. Copyright © 1985 by Beverley Naidoo/British Defence and Aid Fund for South Africa. Reprinted by permission of Harper & Row, Publishers, Inc.

"The Old Woman in the Gourd" from *Folk Tales from Asia for Children Everywhere*, Book Two. Copyright © 1975 by Weatherhill, Inc. Reprinted by permission of Weatherhill, Inc.

The Wright Brothers by Quentin Reynolds. Copyright 1950 by Random House, Inc. Reprinted by permission of the publisher.

"The Practical Princess" from *The Practical Princess and Other Liberating Fairy Tales* by Jay Williams. Copyright © 1978 by Jay Williams. Reprinted by permission of Scholastic Inc.

"Neddy Norris and the Useless Ant-Eater" from *Gargling with Jelly* by Brian Patten. Copyright © 1985 by Brian Patten. Published by Kestrel Books, 1985. Reprinted by permission of Rogers, Coleridge & White Ltd.

Getting Even by Mavis Jukes. Copyright © 1988 by Mavis Jukes. Reprinted by permission of Alfred A. Knopf, Inc.

"Nyangara, the Python" from *The Lion on the Path and Other African Stories* by Hugh Tracey. Copyright © 1968 by Hugh Tracey. Reprinted by permission of Paul Tracey, 340 Las Casas Ave., Pacific Palisades, CA 90272, and Andrew Tracey, International Library of African Music, Rhodes University, Grahamstown 6140, South Africa.

Who's That Girl with the Gun? A Story of Annie Oakley by Robert Quackenbush. Copyright © 1987, 1988. Used by permission of the publisher, Prentice Hall Books for Young Readers, New York, NY 10020.

The Magic Stone translated by Richard and Clara Winston. Text copyright © 1974 by Leonie Kooiker, Papendrecht. Translation copyright © 1978 by William Morrow and Company, Inc. Reprinted by permission of William Morrow and Company, Inc.

"The Hot Pizza Serenade" by Frank Jacobs. Reprinted by permission of *Mad Magazine*, copyright © 1967 by E.C. Publications, Inc.

The Night Swimmers by Betsy Byars. Copyright © 1980 by Betsy Byars. Used by permission of Dell Books, a division of Bantam, Doubleday, Dell Publishing.

"Logic" from *Sweet and Sour: Tales from China* by Carol Kendall and Yao-wen Li. Copyright © 1979 by Seabury Press. Reprinted by permission of Harper & Row, Publishers, Inc.

Contents

Dear Friend,

Because you read the title and looked at the cover of this book, you probably think it's a reading book. Well, you're right!

In this book, you will find a lot of different stories and some activities to do after you've finished reading them. In choosing the stories, I looked for subjects and writing styles that kids I know would find interesting and fun to read. When I wrote the activities, I tried to find ways to help you think about the story. I know that sometimes after you read a story, you just fill in the blanks and close the book. I don't want that to happen here, so I talk directly to you in some of the activities. I might give you clues and ideas for an activity or even a sample to start you off. This way, you and I can work together.

By now, you might be wondering what kind of person wrote this book. I like to do a lot of things. I like to read and write. I like to cook, but I hate to clean up. I like to go barefoot, and I like to wear boots. And if I don't like doing something, I put it off till it can't wait any longer. These are just a few things that tell the kind of person I am. Now here's a picture of me and my two cats to show you what I look like.

Happy reading,

Dotti

INCREDIBLE JOURNEYS

1. Where have you traveled? Think of the names of some places you have visited. Write the names on the lines below.

_____ _____

_____ _____

2. One time when I was traveling around New York City, I used the subway. The train pulled into a station, and the doors opened. There, much to my surprise, stood a friend I hadn't seen in a long, long time. We rode the subway together and talked and talked. That was an incredible journey!

Think about the trips you have taken. Did anything incredible ever happen? What was it?

_____

_____

3. Read this list of events. Which ones would make a journey incredible? Put checks beside them.

_____ rode in a blimp

_____ heard flutes and voices singing

_____ watched the countryside become a blur

_____ crossed a desert by camel

_____ began a 150-mile walk

_____ crossed an ocean in three hours

_____ talked to a fox, a tiger, and some monkeys

_____ flew above the trees

Believe it or not, all those events happen in the stories in this unit. So grab your hat and let's go on some INCREDIBLE JOURNEYS!

Getting Ready to Read

1. I hope you have your toothbrush with you! You're going on a trip, and you may need it.

Complete the ticket below. Decide where and when you are going, how you will travel, and how much the ticket will cost.

```
                    GO-AWAY TRAVEL AGENCY
                    YOUR TOWN, YOUR STATE
TRIP TO:
DATE LEAVING:                      DATE RETURNING:
KIND OF TRANSPORTATION:
COST:
```

2. Lora and Keith dream of flying to the moon. But the cost of going to the moon is currently estimated to be $50,000 per person. Lora and Keith certainly don't have that kind of money! How could they make their trip for no cost at all?

_____

_____

3. By now you've probably decided that you're going to read about transportation. Well, you're right! But before you begin the article on the next page, read the title. Then make a short list of ways people can travel. Put a check by the ones you think will be in the article.

A. *car* _____   **E.** _____

B. _____   **F.** _____

C. _____   **G.** _____

D. _____   **H.** _____

Reading

As you read "From Slow to Fast," answer the questions in the margin.

FROM SLOW *TO FAST*

by Dotti Kauffman

For thousands and thousands of years, the speed at which people traveled did not change. People used footpower to get from place to place. Carrying even a light load, a person could travel only 15 to 20 miles a day.

Then somehow someone learned that waterways could be used as roads. On the very simple early boats, passengers and loads of goods had to be balanced just so. A mistake could prove costly, if not wet. Still, sailing was faster than walking.

At about the same time, traders were learning the fastest way to travel long distances over desert lands. They used camels. These animals traveled at about two and a half miles an hour. Sudden sandstorms or a lame animal might slow them down. But a camel caravan could often get goods to market in half the time it would take for someone to carry them on foot.

What problem did early travelers have?

Now how fast could people travel?

8

What was the next big step in transportation?

What invention finally helped people go faster?

The first wheel was the next big step. Neither the exact time nor the inventor is known. But we do know that by 3500 B.C. or so a solid, round wheel was being used in the lands between the Tigris and Euphrates rivers in the Middle East. It would be another 1,500 years until the spoked wheel was invented. This let cart makers build much lighter wagons that could be pulled by horses. The top speed a person could travel now rose to 15 to 20 miles an hour!

For thousands more years, try as they might, people could not go any faster. Oh, they tried better horses, more horses, and better wagons. And they did put shoes on horses' feet to help them over long distances and hard ground. Nothing really worked, though, until a new source of power was invented: the steam engine. Early engines were slow, going no more than four miles an hour. Yet by the late 1800s, steam engines were whisking their loads along at a hundred miles an hour.

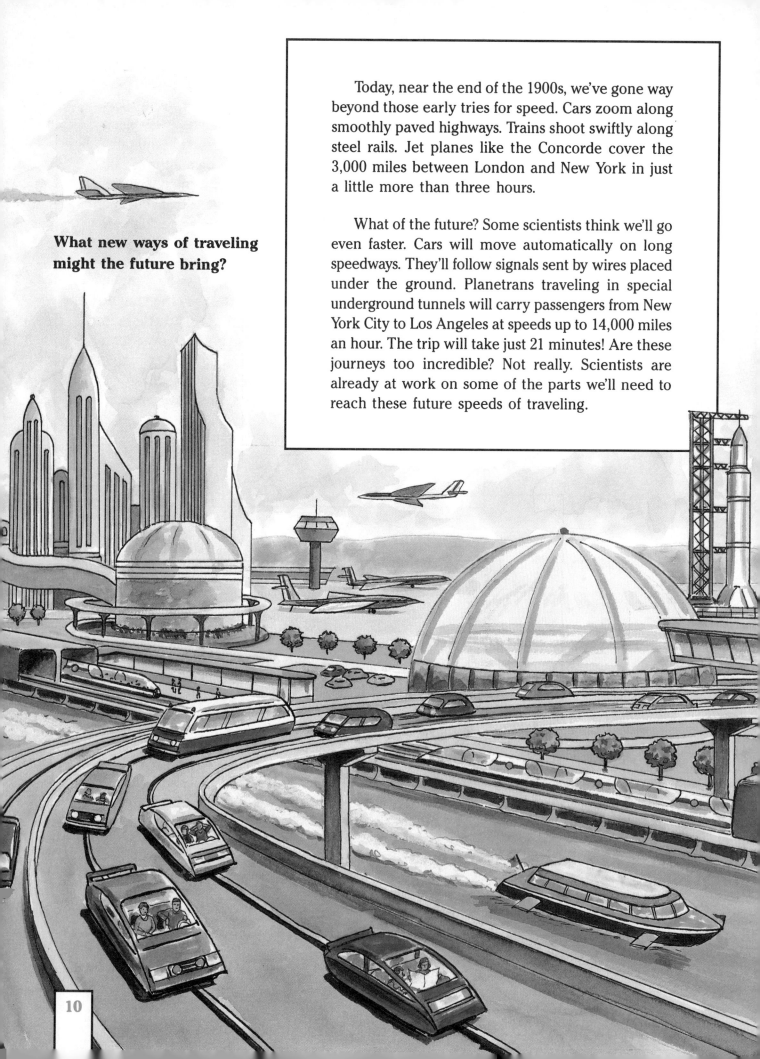

What new ways of traveling might the future bring?

Today, near the end of the 1900s, we've gone way beyond those early tries for speed. Cars zoom along smoothly paved highways. Trains shoot swiftly along steel rails. Jet planes like the Concorde cover the 3,000 miles between London and New York in just a little more than three hours.

What of the future? Some scientists think we'll go even faster. Cars will move automatically on long speedways. They'll follow signals sent by wires placed under the ground. Planetrans traveling in special underground tunnels will carry passengers from New York City to Los Angeles at speeds up to 14,000 miles an hour. The trip will take just 21 minutes! Are these journeys too incredible? Not really. Scientists are already at work on some of the parts we'll need to reach these future speeds of traveling.

Thinking About What You Read

What did you find out?

1. If you had been alive thousands of years ago, would you rather have traveled by land or by water? Why?

_____

_____

2. What was the problem with the first wheel?

_____

_____

3. What pieces of equipment today have solid wheels? Why do they have them?

_____

_____

4. What is the main idea of the last paragraph of the article?

_____

_____

5. What experiences have you had to support that main idea?

_____

_____

How did the author help you read the selection?

When I wrote this article, I wanted you to think about how travel has changed over time. To do this I had to use "time clues," or words that identified time for you.

1. There are no known dates for some of the information. So I sometimes had to use words that described time in general terms. Look at the first sentence of the first paragraph. Find the words that tell you about many, many years. Write them here.

_____

2. Now look at the next two paragraphs. They tell about two different events. But they also tell about the same general period of history. Find the time clues that tell you the two events occurred at about the same time. Write those clues on the hourglass at the right.

3. Now reread the rest of the selection. Find all the clues that tell you when events happened. See how many *different* kinds of time clues you can find and list them below.

_____   _____

_____   _____

_____   _____

_____   _____

How can you use time clues to tell your readers when events happened?

Pretend you lived in one of the time periods in "From Slow to Fast." Then choose an occupation that requires travel. Write a series of daily journal entries for a trip you took. Be sure to use lots of time clues to tell when everything happened. When you're done, share your journal with a friend. Did the time clues make your daily activities clear to your friend?

_____

_____

_____

_____

_____

_____

_____

_____

_____

_____

_____

_____

Getting Ready to Read

1. You know this saying, don't you?

> I SCREAM! YOU SCREAM!
> WE ALL SCREAM FOR ICE CREAM!

I thought you'd know it! Well, what is it about ice cream that makes it so popular? Fill the carton at the right with four words that describe ice cream.

2. Describing ice cream is easy. But what *facts* do you know about it? Write three facts about ice cream below.

☆ _____

☆ _____

☆ _____

3. If you had to prove the facts you just wrote, how would you do it? Would you go to a special place? Where? Why?

_____

_____

_____

4. Now suppose I told you there was a fantastic place you could go to prove your facts. Well, there is. It's the land where ice cream grows. How would you get there? What might you find there to help you prove what you know about ice cream?

_____

_____

_____

Reading

Grab a spoon and let's go to the land where ice cream grows! Read the story that begins on page 14. Answer the questions in the margin while you read.

The Land Where Ice Cream Grows

by Anthony Burgess

Jack and Tom and I were having dinner one day. There was a big, red-faced man sitting alone at the next table, and he'd just finished eating a steak as big as an elephant's ear. The waiter said to him, "Would you like some ice cream now, sir?" The man nearly exploded and said, "Ice cream? I don't want to see ice cream ever ever again!" Naturally, we pricked up our ears at this and we spoke to him. He told us about the land where the ice cream grows and how to find it. "But don't go in a plane," he said. "I had engine trouble and was stuck there six months. Go in a blimp. You can rent one for 523 pongpings a month." So that's what we did.

Why do you think the man never wants to see ice cream again?

14

What did they use to see where to land?

What do you think the three travelers will find?

What did they investigate first?

Here we are within sight of the lovely mountains of chocolate, vanilla and pistachio. As you can see, I kept a dairy, sorry, diary of our expedition.

MUNCHDAY

The cold mouth of evening was beginning to settle on the mountaintops. Then night fell, blueblack and like a great deepfreeze, and we sailed on looking for a level plain to land. We had both our searchlights probing like tongues and soon we found ourselves in an ice cream dessert, sorry, desert, with ice cream cones sticking up like ancient monuments. *Were* they monuments? Did people live here? And if so, what did they live on? There was no sign of a tongue-lick or the scoop of a great spoon anywhere.

CHEWSDAY

At dawn we tied our ship to an ice cream cone. The cone was very well made, but who had made it? Tom said it just grew, like a plant.

The first thing we did was to test the quality of the ice cream under our feet. It was very good and natural, nothing synthetic about it at all, and the taste was of vanilla with a faint glow of blueberry. Jack began to work out how much ice cream there was. But how deep down did it go? There must surely be enough here to feed the whole world.

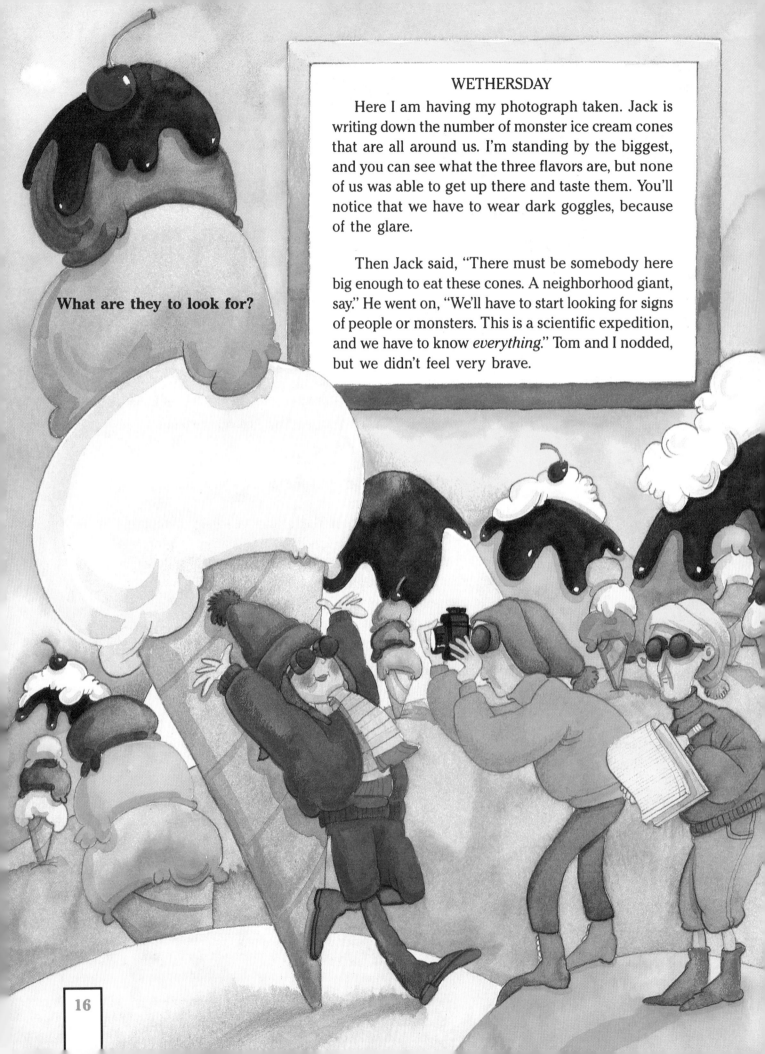

What are they to look for?

WETHERSDAY

Here I am having my photograph taken. Jack is writing down the number of monster ice cream cones that are all around us. I'm standing by the biggest, and you can see what the three flavors are, but none of us was able to get up there and taste them. You'll notice that we have to wear dark goggles, because of the glare.

Then Jack said, "There must be somebody here big enough to eat these cones. A neighborhood giant, say." He went on, "We'll have to start looking for signs of people or monsters. This is a scientific expedition, and we have to know *everything*." Tom and I nodded, but we didn't feel very brave.

Thinking About What You Read

What did you find out?

1. Why did the three brave explorers want to go to the land where ice cream grows?

_____

_____

2. What things could the friends have brought back with them to prove that the land where ice cream grows was real?

_____

_____

3. Which one of those things would have been the best proof of the journey? Why?

_____

_____

How did the author help you read the story?

Mr. Burgess used both facts and opinions about ice cream in this story. He knew, for example, that ice cream is a dessert, comes in different flavors, and can be served in cones. He also knew that most people like ice cream.

The author "flavored" his story, too. He added some tasty morsels that let readers enjoy the subject even more. He described some objects in terms of other things—things they are like.

1. Reread the first paragraph of the story. How big was the steak the red-faced man was eating?

_____

   Do you know how big that is? Well, I don't either, but the actual size isn't important. What is important is that by using these words, Mr. Burgess tells us that the steak was very, VERY big.

2. Now reread "MUNCHDAY." Find the sentence that describes the night. Underline the words that compare the night with something else. How could night in this land be like that?

_____

   Both of these comparisons are called **similes.** Similes are comparisons that use the words *like* or *as.* Writers use similes to help readers see how one thing is like something else. Because similes can be fun, they invite us to enjoy a writer's work.

Mr. Burgess also uses **wordplays** to help us enjoy his writing. A wordplay is simply a witty use of words. Look at the end of the story's second paragraph. Here, Mr. Burgess leads us into a wordplay. He writes "dairy" ("Of course," you say. "That's where ice cream starts!"), but he really wants to lead you to "diary." He allows his subject, ice cream, to flavor his story.

3. Look at "MUNCHDAY" again. Find another sentence where Mr. Burgess plays with the subject and words. Draw a box around the words he plays with. Why does this wordplay work?

_____

How can you use similes and wordplays in your writing?

1. Complete each of these similes.

as creamy as _____   like the crunch _____

as high as _____   like marshmallow _____

2. Mr. Burgess played with words and sounds when he named the first day "Munchday." He joined the words "munch" and "Monday" to make a new word that flavored his story. Can you think of other words that play on the ice cream theme? List your wordplays, either real or imaginary, below. I have started the list for you.

berried (buried)   _____

_____   _____

3. Imagine that you are with the three story characters in the land where ice cream grows. Send a postcard home, telling what is happening on your trip. Use the similes and wordplays you have just written, or any others you can think of.

3 Getting Ready to Read

1. Have you ever watched birds flying? How do they do it?

_____

_____

2. If you wanted to fly like a bird, you would have to make wings. What shape would you give them? How would you arrange the different parts? Draw a design for your wings here.

3. What would be the advantages of having wings like yours?

_____

_____

4. What are some other ways you could fly?

_____

_____

Reading

The poem on page 20 is about a different way to fly. I'll bet you've even used it to visit many a faraway place! What in the world could it be? Write your guess here.

_____

Now read the poem to find out if you were right.

I, Icarus

by Alden Nowlan

There was a time when I could fly. I swear it.
Perhaps, if I think hard for a moment, I can even tell
    you the year.
My room was on the ground floor at the rear of the
    house.
My bed faced a window.
Night after night I lay on my bed and willed myself
    to fly.
It was hard work, I can tell you.
Sometimes I lay perfectly still for an hour before I
    felt my body rising from the bed.
I rose slowly, slowly, until I floated three or four feet
    above the floor.
Then, with a kind of swimming motion, I propelled
    myself toward the window.

Outside, I rose higher and higher, above the pasture
    fence, above the clothesline, above the dark,
    haunted trees beyond the pasture.
And, all the time, I heard the music of the flutes.
It seemed the wind made this music.
And sometimes there were voices singing.
All of this was a long time ago and I cannot remember
    the words the voices sang.
But I know I flew when I heard them.

Thinking About What You Read

What did you find out?

1. At what time of day did the poet fly? Why did he choose that time?

_____

_____

2. How old do you think the poet was when he did his flying? What makes you think so?

_____

_____

3. Why do you think the poet said that the music he heard sounded like flutes?

_____

_____

4. If the poet had flown in bright sunlight, what instrument might have made the music? Why?

_____

_____

5. There is an old Greek story about a boy named Icarus and his father, Daedalus. Daedalus worked for a king, but when he wanted to leave, the king locked him up. So Daedalus built wonderful wings out of feathers and wax for him and Icarus to wear in their escape. They would strap the wings to their backs and fly to freedom. Now Daedalus had cautioned Icarus not to fly too close to the sun because its heat would melt the wax on his wings. But the sheer joy of flying was too great, and Icarus forgot his father's warning. When he soared high in the air, up near the sun, the wax did indeed melt. Icarus fell to his death in the sea. Why do you think the poet chose "I, Icarus" as the title for his poem?

_____

_____

_____

6. Why is this poem in a unit called INCREDIBLE JOURNEYS?

_____

_____

How did the poet help you read the poem?

When Mr. Nowlan wrote this poem, he wanted his readers to follow him in his flight. But how did the poet make us feel like we were with him? He started the trip inside the house and described exactly where he was and where everything around him was. Then he moved outside and took us with him, from the ground up into the night sky. Now let's look at how Mr. Nowlan organized his information by the order of his descriptions.

First, go back and number the lines of Mr. Nowlan's poem. Write the numbers in the margin to the left of all the lines that begin with capital letters.

1. Now look at line 1. What part of this line tells you what the whole poem will be about? Underline the words.

2. Next, look at lines 3–6. How do these lines set the stage for what is to come?

_____

_____

3. Now look at line 8. How did the trip begin? Underline the important words in this sentence.

4. Reread the rest of the poem. Underline the parts that tell you about the trip.

5. One way to see how Mr. Nowlan leads his readers is to draw the series of events that he describes. This series of pictures could be the outline for a planned filmstrip of this poem. Complete the frames below to show how the poet's trip took place. Look back at the poem to find out what you want in each frame. I've started the filmstrip for you. You need to decide where the poet is at the end of the poem.

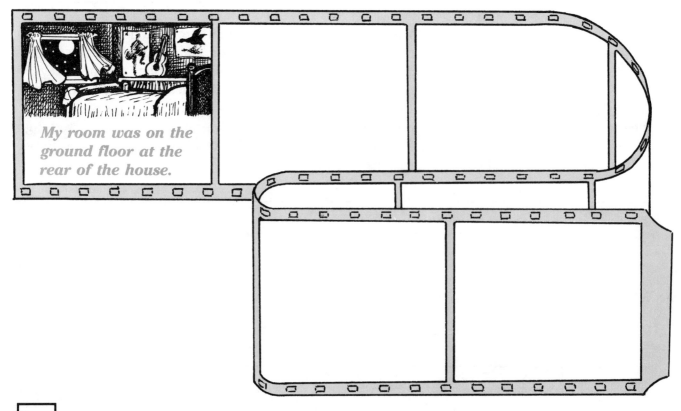

My room was on the ground floor at the rear of the house.

How can you organize information to show readers where things happen?

Think about a dream you've had in which you traveled somewhere. List the places you went in the order you visited them.

_____   _____

_____   _____

_____   _____

_____   _____

Now write a short story or poem to describe your dream. Help the reader keep you company as you move from place to place. Give your story or poem a good title.

_____

_____

_____

_____

_____

_____

_____

_____

_____

_____

_____

_____

_____

_____

_____

_____

Getting Ready to Read

1. Going on a journey is nothing new to most people. We've done it many times. Going away is often just a small, though exciting, part of our lives. Now think about your family and your classmates. How many of them have gone on journeys? How did they travel? Complete the chart below to show how many of your family (**F**) and classmates (**C**) have used each way of traveling given at the bottom.

	F	C	F	C	F	C	F	C	F	C
Everyone										
About half of them										
Only a few of them										
None of them										
	car		train		bus		plane		on foot	

2. Now look again at your chart. Which way of traveling has been used least of all?

_____

If you traveled in this way, what might your journey be like? What problems and dangers might you face? What would be incredible about traveling this way?

_____

_____

_____

3. Look quickly at the story title on the next page. What could be incredible about that kind of journey?

_____

_____

Reading

Now read the story that begins on page 25 to find out just why this journey was incredible for Tiro and Naledi. Answer the questions in the margin while you read.

RIDE ON A TRUCK

by
Beverley Naidoo

**Where did the children
spend the night?**

Tiro woke when he heard the rooster crow. The shed was already half light. He shook Naledi. "Get up! We must hurry!"

As they crept out from the shed, they saw the farm buildings a little distance away, with thick smoke rising from the chimney.

Silently they ran through the long grass toward the orange trees. Then through the orange trees, row after row, until there at last was the barbed wire.

Finding the road again, they felt almost happy! The road was cool from the night and they sang as they walked.

The sun rose higher. On they walked. The heat sank into them and they felt the sweat on their bodies. On they walked. Alone again, except for the odd flashing by of a car or a truck.

SCREECH! Tires skidded and stopped.

"Where are you two kids going?"

The driver of the truck stuck a friendly face out the window.

"To Johannesburg, Rra."

What do you think screeched to a stop?

26

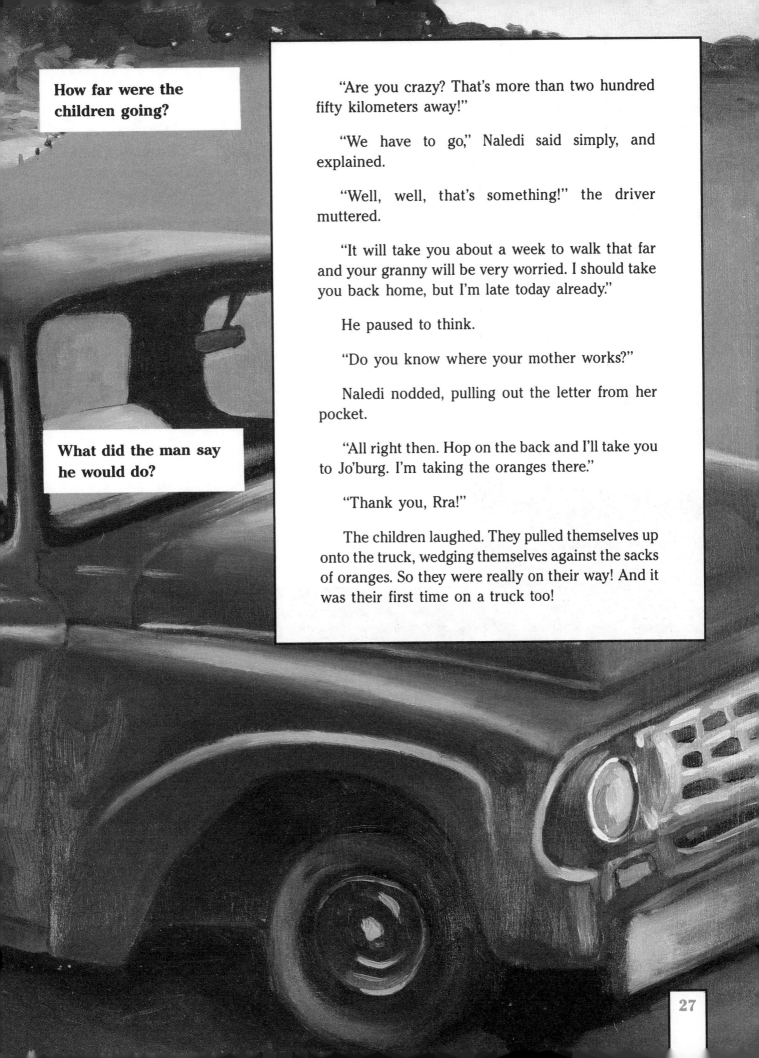

How far were the children going?

What did the man say he would do?

"Are you crazy? That's more than two hundred fifty kilometers away!"

"We have to go," Naledi said simply, and explained.

"Well, well, that's something!" the driver muttered.

"It will take you about a week to walk that far and your granny will be very worried. I should take you back home, but I'm late today already."

He paused to think.

"Do you know where your mother works?"

Naledi nodded, pulling out the letter from her pocket.

"All right then. Hop on the back and I'll take you to Jo'burg. I'm taking the oranges there."

"Thank you, Rra!"

The children laughed. They pulled themselves up onto the truck, wedging themselves against the sacks of oranges. So they were really on their way! And it was their first time on a truck too!

How was riding different from walking?

What almost happened?

The engine started up and the lorry was soon thundering along. Walking had been so quiet, but traveling in a lorry was very noisy. The air, which had been so hot and still before, now swept by their faces. The land, which had stood still, now seemed to rush by.

Thornbushes, telegraph poles, wire fences, plowed fields, cattle, rows of oranges, tall gum trees by a farm house . . . Almost as soon as they had seen something, it was gone.

Little by little, Tiro began to lean farther out over the side to feel the wind on his face. Naledi called, "Sit back or you'll fall!" but her brother took no notice.

Suddenly the truck went over a bump and Tiro jerked forward. Naledi grabbed him just in time.

"Didn't I tell you?" she shouted over the noise of the lorry.

A little shaken, Tiro mumbled "Sorry" and settled back properly against the orange sacks. Together they watched the road stretching far out behind them.

Thinking About What You Read

What did you find out?

1. What time of day was it when Tiro and Naledi left the shed? How do you know?

_____

_____

2. What time of day was it when the truck driver offered them a ride? How do you know?

_____

_____

3. How did Naledi and Tiro's feelings about their journey change from the beginning of the story to the end?

_____

_____

How did the author help you read the story?

In some parts of her story, Ms. Naidoo wants you to read slowly and calmly. In other parts, she wants you to read quickly and to feel excitement. How does she get her readers to do this?

Reread the first two paragraphs of the story. The first paragraph calmly gives you information. Put a plus sign (+) in the margin beside it. The second paragraph gives you a feeling of speed and excitement. Put a minus sign (−) beside it.

Now let's look at the sentences in these two paragraphs. The first paragraph has longer sentences than the second. All of the sentences in the first paragraph end with periods, too. As you know, periods usually end statements. Statements simply give you information. They don't excite you.

The second paragraph, though, has only two short sentences. Both of them end with exclamation marks. You already know that exclamation marks signal great feeling or excitement. We tend to read short, exclamatory sentences very quickly.

So Ms. Naidoo uses longer sentences ending with periods when she wants you to read slowly and calmly. But when she wants you to read quickly and to feel excitement, she uses short sentences ending with exclamation marks.

1. Reread paragraphs 3–5 of the story. Look at the length of the sentences and mark each paragraph with a **+** or a **−**.

2. Now look at the sixth paragraph. This one is a bit trickier. Should it have a **+** or a **−**? Both? Why?

_____

_____

How can you use sentences of different lengths to make your readers speed up or slow down?

Imagine you are Tiro and Naledi. You've just been dropped off at the edge of Jo'burg, and you've never seen such a large, busy city before. What sights, sounds, and smells would be familiar? Which of them would be new, exciting, or even dangerous? On the lines below, write a short story to describe your walk into Jo'burg. Try to use both long and short sentences to make your readers understand what you're experiencing.

_____

_____

_____

_____

_____

_____

_____

_____

_____

_____

_____

_____

_____

_____

_____

_____

_____

Now give your story to a friend. Ask your friend to mark your paragraphs with the **+** or **−** signs we used earlier. Then see how well you used short and long sentences to make your readers understand what was happening.

Getting Ready to Read

1. There's a saying, "A promise made is a debt unpaid." What does this saying mean?

_____

_____

2. Read this list of promises. Put a check beside those you have made and kept.

_____ I promise to be home in time to eat.   _____ I promise not to fight anymore.

_____ I promise to do all my homework.   _____ I promise to keep my room clean.

Now write one more promise that you have made and really kept.

_____

3. Why do people make promises and then break them?

_____

_____

4. "The Old Woman in the Gourd" is a folktale about a woman who makes some promises while on a journey to visit her daughter. From your earlier reading of folktales, what kinds of characters would you expect to meet in this one?

_____

_____

In folktales, how many times do characters often have similar things happen to them?

_____

Reading

Read the story that begins on page 32. When you reach the old woman's first promise, underline it. Decide whether she will keep or break the promise and write *keep* or *break* beside the part you underlined. Then finish the story to see if you were right. Answer the questions in the margin while you read.

Long, long ago an old woman set out to visit her married daughter who had gone to live some distance away.

By and by she came to a thick forest and there she met a fox. "Old woman, I have been without food for ten days," said the fox. "You can go no farther, for I shall eat you up!"

"Be patient, dear fox," said the old woman. "I am going to see my daughter, but in a month I shall be coming back this way, so please let me go. I am thin now, but then I shall be fat and you can eat me as soon as you like."

"A fat woman would make a better meal than a thin one," thought the fox, so he let her go. She hurried away, hoping that no one else would try to stop her.

She had not gone far when the ferocious king of the forest, the tiger, appeared and snarled: "Old woman, I have been hungry for twenty days. You will make a meal for me—be prepared to die!"

"Please let me go, O King of Beasts," said the old woman. "You can eat me when I come back from visiting my daughter at the end of a month. By then I'll be fat and tasty, not thin and tough as I am now."

So the tiger let her go.

How many times has the woman made a promise? Do you think she will make any more?

Before long the King of Monkeys, with all his tribe, stood in her way. To deceive her, he greeted her politely with a garland of sweet-smelling flowers. Then he said with a grin: "Old woman, you have come just in time. I shall have pleasure in eating you."

"Be patient, O Lord of Monkeys," said the old woman. "I am on my way to visit my daughter, so please let me go. I am thin now, but in a month I'll be fat and then you can eat me as soon as you like."

But the King of Monkeys was not as easily tricked as the fox and the tiger. At his command a regiment of monkeys surrounded her, shrieking and screaming. The little ones even dared to climb up onto her shoulders and jump on her head.

She begged and prayed them to let her go, but the King of Monkeys said: "I shall not believe you are really coming back this way unless you swear by the Buddha!"

The old woman had to take the oath, and then she was allowed to go on her way. At long last she reached her daughter's house and stayed there happily. But the time flew by and the end of the month came all too soon. Then she remembered her promise to the animals and told her daughter all about it. They put their heads together and made a plan. The daughter brought two big gourds. One was a Lanka, which is shaped like a bottle, and the other was a Chinda, shaped like a snake. The daughter put the old woman inside the Lanka and asked the Chinda to lead the way. Thus they came into the forest where the monkeys, the tiger, and the fox were waiting hungrily for the old woman.

At the crossroads the monkeys were gathered, growing more suspicious every moment. Suddenly they heard a strange rattling sound and saw the Chinda approaching, followed by the big Lanka.

"Make way for us!" called the Chinda loudly. "What do you mean by blocking our way like this?"

Taken aback by this unexpected challenge, the King of Monkeys said politely: "We were just waiting for an old woman who has promised to be our dinner. As you came along did you see her by any chance?"

"What business have we with your old woman?" said the Chinda haughtily. "Out of our way!" And the Chinda and the Lanka rattled on.

Will the old woman keep her promise to the animals?

Will the trick work?

Soon they came to the place where the tiger was waiting. He was determined not to listen to a single word from the old woman this time but to pounce on her and gobble her up at once.

First there came a strange sound and then the tiger saw the Chinda rolling toward him followed by the rocking Lanka.

"Make way for us!" shouted the Chinda.

Bewildered, the tiger stepped out of the way; then suddenly remembering, he said: "Oh, have you seen the old woman who promised to be my dinner?"

"What business have we with your old woman?" said the Chinda. "Out of our way!" And the Chinda and the Lanka passed on.

By this time the fox had heard about the strange carriage that was rolling through the forest and he was very suspicious. So he placed a sharp-edged stone in the middle of the pathway. Then he hid behind a tree and waited.

By and by, here came the Chinda and the Lanka at a great speed. The old woman was chuckling to herself at the clever way they had tricked the monkeys and the tiger.

"Crack!" The Lanka hit the sharp stone and split from top to bottom, throwing the old woman onto the path.

What did the fox put in the pathway?

35

What did the woman suggest the animals do?

What do you think the woman's plan is?

Now, the monkeys and the tiger had soon realized the trick that had been played on them and were pursuing the Lanka. Just as the fox was about to eat the old woman all by himself, the other animals came racing up.

The old woman knew that she was caught this time, but she hadn't given up hope yet. She agreed that the animals should eat her, but said: "It would be wise to roast me first. I shall taste better that way."

So the animals made a fire to roast her. "The fire must turn to ashes before it is ready; then I shall be cooked in no time," said the old woman, hoping to delay them still further.

When at last the fire turned to ashes, the old woman took a stone and sat on it in the middle of the heap. The animals, thinking their meal would soon be ready, closed their eyes and made their customary prayer.

Quickly the old woman scooped up some ashes and threw them in the animals' faces so that they were blinded. Before they could recover, she ran out of the forest and escaped.

Furiously angry and very hungry, the fox, the tiger, and the King of Monkeys searched everywhere for the old woman. But they never saw her again.

Thinking About What You Read

What did you find out?

1. Which animal seemed smartest? Why?

_____

_____

_____

2. What might have happened if the old woman had met the fox first on her return journey?

_____

_____

_____

3. If you were one of the animals, how would you feel at the end of the story?

_____

_____

4. Have you read another folktale or fairy tale that has some things in it that remind you of this one? What is the tale? In what ways are the two tales similar?

_____

_____

_____

How did the author help you read the story?

1. As you started to read the story, everything seemed to happen in the way you expected. You already know that folktales have certain features. Which of them were in this story?

_____

_____

_____

2. You also know that writers use quotation marks to set off the words people say. Look at the beginning of the story. Find a place where the writer used quotation marks to set off the fox's words. Underline the words the fox said.

3. Now locate the words the tiger spoke. Look closely at how these words are written. What punctuation appears just before the quotation marks?

_____

Underline the tiger's words and the punctuation mark that comes before them.

4. Scan the story and find other places where colons introduce quotations. Underline those quotations.

_____

What seems to be alike in all the quotations that are introduced by a colon?

_____

_____

5. How could you rewrite the second paragraph of the story so that a colon introduces the fox's words?

_____

_____

_____

_____

How can you use colons to introduce long or formal quotations?

Think back to the part of the story where the King of Monkeys made the old woman take an oath. Write two new sentences for the story. Write new words for the King of Monkeys to say when he made the old woman swear an oath. Then write words for the old woman to say in response. Introduce each long or formal quotation with a colon.

_____

_____

_____

_____

_____

_____

_____

_____

JUST REWARDS

Congratulations! You have just been named to be on the Just Rewards Committee. The committee gives five awards each year. Your job is to decide what each award is given for and who should win it.

**Award for
Bravery**

Awarded for _____

Given to _____

**Award for
Creativity**

Awarded for _____

Given to _____

**Award for Following
the Golden Rule**

Awarded for _____

Given to _____

**Award for Using
Common Sense**

Awarded for _____

Given to _____

**Award for Playing
the Best Trick**

Awarded for _____

Given to _____

1. Select your award winners from the following five choices. Then fill out the awards.

a princess   a colony of ants   a college student   two brothers   a group of children

2. In addition to the paper awards, what other rewards might these winners get?

_____   _____

_____   _____

All of your award winners are in the stories in this unit. But just what do they have to do with JUST REWARDS? Well, put on your judge's robe and let's go find out!

Getting Ready to Read

1. Is there something you'd like to learn to do? What is it?

_____

2. How can you teach yourself to do something new? Make a list of some ways you can learn a new skill. I have written one idea to get you started.

watch a tape about it

_____   _____

_____   _____

_____   _____

3. Suppose that you have now done one or more of the things you listed for question 2. You know at least the basics of how to do your new skill. Which two actions below might be the most rewarding second and third things to do? Write *2* and *3* next to your choices to show the order of what you'd do.

_____ Collect photos of other people doing the skill.   _____ Talk about the skill with my friends.

_____ Go out and try to do my new skill.   _____ Gather all the things I need to do the skill.

4. If you were the first person ever to do something, what rewards would you expect? List two or three of them here.

_____   _____

_____   _____

5. You probably know that Wilbur and Orville Wright were the first people to fly successfully. How do you think they learned to fly? Could they have used any of the ways you listed in question 2? Put a star by each answer to question 2 that the Wrights could have used.

6. What is one special reward the Wright brothers might have expected for being the first to fly?

_____

Reading

Read the story that begins on page 41 to learn more about the Wright brothers. Answer the questions in the margin while you read.

Kitty Hawk

by Quentin Reynolds

Why did the Wrights choose Kitty Hawk?

Today you could get on an airplane at Dayton and be at Kitty Hawk in about three hours. But it took Wilbur and Orv a week to reach the lonely fishing hamlet. Kitty Hawk is about sixty miles from Cape Hatteras, which is one of the stormiest places on the Atlantic coast. But it isn't stormy at Kitty Hawk. It is a place of sand dunes and gentle hills and no trees at all.

"This is perfect," Wilbur said. "And best of all, there are scarcely any people here. Nobody will think we're crazy when we start flying our glider."

They had brought a tent with them and they put it up. Kate had packed a suitcase with jelly and jam and other things she always "put up" at home. Will and Orv had brought all of their precious books and pamphlets and all kinds of tools with them, and now they were ready for the big test.

What was the glider made of?

Who do you think will be the first to ride?

How did they choose who would ride?

Kitty Hawk, the scene of their test, consisted of nothing but a government weather bureau and a life-saving station, but because of these it had a post office. This was run by Mr. William Tate, and Will and Orv arranged with Mrs. Tate to have their meals with the family.

As they assembled their glider there was no one to laugh at them but a few seagulls hovering above. The glider was just a big box kite with an upper and a lower wing. Mr. Tate (who only had four or five letters a day to deliver) looked at it curiously, but he didn't laugh. There was something about these two serious-eyed young men that kept a person from laughing. Mr. Tate, in fact, asked if he could help them.

Well, they needed a helper. They had reached the point where they had "studied the way to ride a horse," and now they had to climb on its back and see if they could stay on. One of them would ride on the glider, but two others were needed to run along with it and give it a start. This glider had to be pulled along just as a kite was pulled along, until the wind grabbed it and took it up into the air. They tossed a coin and Orville won. He'd be the first rider.

Otto Lilienthal and the other glider experts always sat upright on the lower wing of the gliders. Wilbur remembered the first time his mother had used the expression, "wind resistance," and he remembered how fast his sled had gone when he had lain on it. And of course he remembered how fast Orville had gone on his bike when he had lowered the handle bars and leaned over to "duck the wind."

Why did Orv lie down on the wing?

"Lie down on the wing, Orv," Will said. "That'll reduce the wind resistance."

Orv nodded and took his place. The glider was nestling on top of a sand dune. Wilbur and Mr. Tate stood on either side of it. Wilbur had attached strong cords to each side of the glider, and he and Mr. Tate grabbed the loose ends.

Do you think Orv will succeed on his first try?

"We'll pull the glider downhill," Will explained to Mr. Tate. "And then . . . well . . . maybe it'll go up into the air. Ready? One . . . two . . . three . . . GO!"

They trotted down the sand dune, pulling the light glider along. Nothing happened. They ran now, faster and faster, and suddenly there was a yell from Orville.

Why did Orville yell?

"I'm flying," he cried, and sure enough, the glider was about five feet off the ground.

Thinking About What You Read

What did you find out?

1. How do you think the Wright brothers felt about their successful flight?

_____

_____

Do you think that was a just reward for their efforts? Why or why not?

_____

_____

_____

2. What do you suppose made the Wright brothers want to fly in the first place?

_____

_____

_____

3. How do you think Wilbur felt when he lost the coin toss? Why?

_____

_____

_____

How do you think Orville felt when he won the coin toss? Why?

_____

_____

_____

4. How do you think Mr. Tate felt when the glider lifted off into the air? Why?

_____

_____

_____

5. How would knowing about the Wright brothers' first attempt at flying help another person learn to fly?

_____

_____

_____

_____

How did the author help you read the story?

History books report that the Wright brothers chose Kitty Hawk, North Carolina, for their first attempt at a glider flight. Other records list the items Wilbur and Orville took along and the people who helped them. Mr. Reynolds used all of these kinds of records when he did his research for this biography.

Mr. Reynolds's story isn't filled with facts alone, though. He told the story as if he were there and knew a lot about the Wrights. The result is a story that is friendly and interesting to read.

One way the author helped make his story interesting was by using familiar expressions or sayings. He did that to give readers a very clear idea of his meaning. To make these sayings stand out, Mr. Reynolds put them in quotation marks.

1. There's an example of this kind of saying in the paragraph that tells why the Wrights needed a helper. Find this paragraph and underline the words shown in quotation marks. Then write in your own words what this expression means.

_____

_____

_____

2. The paragraph that mentions other glider experts contains two more familiar expressions. Write each one below. Then tell in your own words what each expression means.

Expression A: _____

Meaning: _____

_____

Expression B: _____

Meaning: _____

_____

How can you use familiar expressions to help your readers understand your meaning?

Now imagine that you are the host of a TV talk show. You are interviewing Orville Wright about his flight. What questions would you ask? What answers might Orville give? On the lines below, write a script for your interview. Use familiar expressions in your questions and in Orville's answers. When you have finished, get a friend to help you read the script aloud.

Getting Ready to Read

What's this? You're going to hire a princess? Lucky you! Having a princess around the house should be fun. But you have to be sure you get the right kind. I suggest you try to find a practical princess.

1. What kind of form would you want a princess to fill out to apply for the job? I've started the form below for you. Add some other things you'd need to know about the princess before you hired her.

Name _____

Age _____

_____

_____

_____

_____

_____

_____

_____

_____

_____

_____

2. Now you've written down all the things you want to know about your princess. Go back and fill in the form the way you think a perfect practical princess would.

3. Boy, she really has great skills! Surely she'll get the job. But wait! Use the Rating Scale for Princesses on the next page, too.

Think about the qualities the perfect practical princess should have as you read the scale. How important are each of these qualities? Using a scale of *1* to *5*, circle the number of points the perfect practical princess would get for each quality. Then total the points your princess receives.

RATING SCALE FOR PRINCESSES

	Least Important			Most Important	
Dresses at all times as a beautiful princess should	1	2	3	4	5
Thinks before she acts	1	2	3	4	5
Uses correct formal English at all times	1	2	3	4	5
Would never kiss a frog	1	2	3	4	5
Is beautiful	1	2	3	4	5
Asks for advice from her elders	1	2	3	4	5
Minds her own business	1	2	3	4	5
Gets servants to do everything for her	1	2	3	4	5
Dances gracefully	1	2	3	4	5
Gives orders in a nice way	1	2	3	4	5
Is charming	1	2	3	4	5
Uses common sense to solve problems	1	2	3	4	5
Is brave	1	2	3	4	5
Never eats apples given to her by old women	1	2	3	4	5
Will marry only a handsome prince	1	2	3	4	5

Total score _____

Reading

Now read the story that begins on the next page. As you read, think about how Princess Bedelia would rate on your scale. Answer the questions in the margin while you read.

The Practical Princess

by Jay Williams

What was unusual about the third fairy's gift?

What did Bedelia's father think of this gift?

Princess Bedelia was as lovely as the moon shining upon a lake full of waterlilies. She was as graceful as a cat leaping. And she was also extremely practical.

When she was born, three fairies had come to her cradle to give her gifts as was usual in that country. The first fairy had given her beauty. The second had given her grace. But the third, who was a wise old creature, had said, "I give her common sense."

"I don't think much of that gift," said King Ludwig, raising his eyebrows. "What good is common sense to a princess? All she needs is charm."

Nevertheless, when Bedelia was eighteen years old, something happened which made the king change his mind.

A dragon moved into the neighborhood. He settled in a dark cave on top of a mountain, and the first thing he did was to send a message to the king. "I must have a princess to devour," the message said, "or I shall breathe out my fiery breath and destroy the kingdom."

Sadly, King Ludwig called together his councillors and read them the message. "Perhaps," said the Prime Minister, "we had better advertise for a knight to slay the dragon? That is what is generally done in these cases."

"I'm afraid we haven't time," answered the king. "The dragon has only given us until tomorrow morning. There is no help for it. We shall have to send him the princess." Princess Bedelia had come to the meeting because, as she said, she liked to mind her own business and this was certainly her business.

What do you think they'll do about the dragon?

What does the king say they must do?

Who must solve the problem?

What do you think she'll do?

"Rubbish!" she said. "Dragons can't tell the difference between princesses and anyone else. Use your common sense. He's just asking for me because he's a snob."

"That may be so," said her father, "but if we don't send you along, he'll destroy the kingdom."

"Right!" said Bedelia. "I see I'll have to deal with this myself." She left the council chamber. She got the largest and gaudiest of her state robes and stuffed it with straw, and tied it together with string. Into the center of the bundle she packed about a hundred pounds of gunpowder. She got two strong young men to carry it up the mountain for her. She stood in front of the dragon's cave, and called, "Come out! Here's the princess!"

The dragon came blinking and peering out of the darkness. Seeing the bright robe covered with gold and silver embroidery, and hearing Bedelia's voice, he opened his mouth wide.

At Bedelia's signal, the two young men swung the robe and gave it a good heave, right down the dragon's throat. Bedelia threw herself flat on the ground, and the two young men ran.

As the gunpowder met the flames inside the dragon, there was a tremendous explosion.

Bedelia got up, dusting herself off. "Dragons," she said, "are not very bright."

What happened?

Thinking About What You Read

What did you find out?

1. Now go back to the Rating Scale for Princesses that you completed before you read the story. Use a different color pencil and rate Princess Bedelia. What is her total score?

_____

2. How does Bedelia compare to your perfect practical princess? Would you hire her? Why or why not?

_____

_____

_____

3. What would you have done to solve Bedelia's problem?

_____

_____

_____

4. Did this fairy tale end like other fairy tales you've read? How was it different?

_____

_____

_____

5. Originally, Bedelia's father didn't think much of the gift of common sense. How do you think he felt about it after Bedelia took care of the dragon? Why?

_____

_____

_____

6. The dragon, of course, got his just reward in this story. But Bedelia got a just reward, too. What was it?

_____

_____

How did the author help you read the story?

I think Mr. Williams's story is really great! I particularly like the fact that his bravest, smartest (and most practical!) character is a girl. In a lot of other stories, boys are the smartest, the bravest, the most heroic, or have the most common sense. This story is good because it's different.

The author made his story different in two ways. Both of those ways involved playing with **stereotypes.** Stereotypes describe people who fit the patterns we expect them to fit. Stereotypical characters look and behave as we think they will.

In this story, Bedelia doesn't quite fit our stereotype of a princess, does she? Aren't story princesses usually pretty helpless? Well, Bedelia is anything but helpless! This is one way Mr. Williams plays with stereotypes.

To make Bedelia seem so strong and smart, Mr. Williams had to make the other characters fit our stereotypes. They had to look and act just as we expected them to. By comparison, Bedelia was a wonder woman! This was another way the author played with stereotypes.

1. How do dragons look and behave in stories? Check the stereotypical features and qualities below that you might expect. Then add a few more features to the list.

_____ are small   _____ are mean   _____ live in caves   _____ eat vegetables

_____   _____

_____   _____

2. Now list some stereotypical features and qualities of kings. Write them below the crown.

_____   _____

_____   _____

Did King Ludwig have any of those features and qualities? Put a star by any features King Ludwig shared.

Mr. Williams's dragon and king were stereotypical. Bedelia wasn't. This helped us to enjoy Bedelia's character, and the story, much more.

How can you use stereotypes to make your writing more interesting?

1. How do witches usually look and behave in stories? List some of their stereotypical features and qualities.

_____   _____

_____   _____

2. Now write a short story about a witch and a just reward. Make your witch different in one or more ways from what your readers might expect. Play with the stereotypes of your other characters, too. Give your story a good title.

_____

_____

_____

_____

_____

_____

_____

_____

_____

_____

_____

_____

_____

_____

_____

_____

_____

_____

Getting Ready to Read

1. Let's go on a picnic! We can take lots of yummy things to eat. M-m-m-m-m! In the space below, draw a picnic scene. Put in all the things you usually find at a picnic.

I wonder—did you put some ants in your picture? You know there are ALWAYS ants at picnics. If you didn't draw them already, go back and add some.

2. Now the picture is complete. Everyone is having a good time, even the ants! Make a list of three things these ants would like about this picnic and three things they would NOT like.

Things Ants Would Like   Things Ants Would Not Like

_____   _____

_____   _____

_____   _____

3. Sometimes when we hear a person's name, we get an idea about the kind of person he or she will turn out to be. The title of the poem you are going to read is "Neddy Norris and the Useless Ant-Eater." What would someone named *Neddy Norris* be like? Why do you think so? What do you think is going to happen to Neddy?

_____

_____

_____

Reading

It's time to find out what REALLY happens to Neddy Norris. Read the poem that begins on the next page. You might be surprised by the ending!

Neddy Norris and the Useless Ant-Eater

by Brian Patten

It was two days after the picnic
On which Neddy tortured the ants
That the ghost of the first one haunted him
By climbing up his pants.

The next day a second ant
Bit him on the toe,
The day after this another
Decided to have a go.

There must have been six thousand ants
And the ghost of each one swore
It would nibble Neddy Norris
Till Neddy Norris was no more.

Neddy went into a pet shop
And he bought a tame ant-eater.
He thought with glee: "Now I'll be safe,
And life will be much sweeter."

The ant-eater was rather placid—
Though it saw what was going on
It stared at the ants as they marched past
Without eating a single one.

Neddy continued to be bitten,
He howled and made a din.
His family grew fed up
And threw him in the bin.

Now the ghostly voice of Neddy Norris
Moans at the failure of his plan.
For he never guessed the ant-eater
Was a vegetarian.

Thinking About What You Read

What did you find out?

1. Did Neddy get a just reward from the ants' ghosts? Why or why not?

_____

_____

_____

2. Neddy thought that an ant-eater would get rid of the ants for him. But what other ways might Neddy have used to get rid of the ants? What could have gone wrong with each way he used? Write your ideas in the lists below.

Ways to Get Rid of Ants	What Could Go Wrong
_____	_____
_____	_____

3. You've probably heard the saying, "Do unto others as you would have them do unto you." How does this saying fit this poem?

_____

_____

_____

How did the poet help you read the poem?

1. The first verse of the poem is reworded below. What's wrong with it?

> The day was two days after the picnic
> On the day Neddy Norris tortured the ants
> That the ghost of the first ant haunted Neddy Norris
> By climbing up Neddy Norris's pants.

_____

_____

If you said this version is awkward and hard to follow because too many nouns are repeated, you're absolutely right! When Mr. Patten wrote this poem, he knew he didn't want to repeat the same nouns over and over again every time he told about Neddy, the ants, or the ant-eater. He also knew he could use **pronouns,** or words that take the place of nouns.

2. Reread the <u>real</u> poem. Make a list of the different pronouns you find. I've started you off.

It _____   _____   _____

_____   _____   _____

_____   _____   _____

3. Now that you've had a chance to compare the real poem with the silly verse in question 1, what can you say pronouns do for us?

_____

How can you use pronouns to make your writing interesting?

An **epitaph** is a short statement or saying about someone who has died. We usually see epitaphs on tombstones. Some of them are funny.

Look at the ant graveyard below. Each tombstone marks the grave of an ant that Neddy Norris tortured. Some tombstones already have epitaphs written on them, but three don't. Write funny epitaphs on the three tombstones. Remember to include pronouns in your epitaphs.

UNCLE NAT ANT
Born ////, Died ////
I once was an uncle,
But now I'm not even
an ant!

BUGSY "LEGS" ANT
Born ////, Died ////
He was squashed
like a bug
By a big HUMAN
thug.

R. MEE ANT
Born ////, Died ////
_____
_____
_____
_____

AUNT ENNA ANT
Born ////, Died ////
She was a gentle soul,
Loved by many a niece,
Till Neddy came along,
and made her
REST IN PEACE.

IMA "RED" ANT
Born ////, Died ////
_____
_____
_____
_____

JUSTRY WARD ANT
Born ////, Died ////
_____
_____
_____
_____

Getting Ready to Read

1. Look at the pictures below. Who would do such things? On each picture frame, write the name of someone you know who might do the thing pictured.

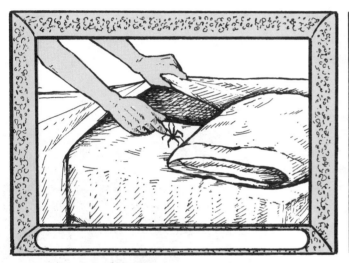

2. What's the best trick you ever played on anyone?

_____

_____

3. What did the person you tricked do to "get even" with you?

_____

_____

4. Why do people play tricks on each other? Make a list of reasons. I've started your list for you.

to surprise someone

_____   _____

_____   _____

_____   _____

Reading

The story that begins on page 62 is about a fifth grader named Maggie. Maggie has a problem with a classmate. Read the story and then decide what Maggie should do. Answer the questions in the margin while you read.

GETTING EVEN

by Mavis Jukes

"Sick!" she cried. She frowned at a hair stuck to the bottom of the bowl. "Everything has hair in it!"

"Oh, come on, now. Don't exaggerate," said her father. He put his hand on his chest. "And pardon me. Next time, fix your own cereal."

"Listen," said Maggie. "Nobody's exaggerating. Every weekend when I'm here, Blossom sneaks up onto my bed at home and gets dog hair all over my pillow."

"Well, I can't be held responsible for what happens at your mother's house. But why don't you shut your bedroom door?"

Maggie didn't answer. "Plus," she continued, "on Friday, Corky Newton put hair in my sandwich."

Her father made a face. "Why did you let him do that?"

"Let him?" said Maggie. "*Let* him? Nobody let him, Dad. He did it when I wasn't looking."

"Then how do you know he was the one who did it?"

"Dad, some things you just know. He always does things like that to people. Of course, he's the principal's nephew, so naturally I can never get even with him. And he's a sneak! I can't catch him at anything! If I try, he just threatens to report me. He's the clean-up captain."

"Report you for what?"

"For anything. How do I know?"

"He's the clean-up captain, and he puts hair in people's lunches?"

"Yes."

Maggie's father picked up the newspaper and turned a page. "Well, I think that's highly inappropriate—it's an abuse of power."

Maggie said nothing.

"And," said her father from behind the newspaper, "I think he needs a taste of his own medicine."

Maggie said nothing.

Her father folded down one corner of the newspaper and looked at her. "You need to get even with him."

"Look, Dad," said Maggie. "The guy's a foot taller than I am. And he's an animal—he can kick a ball over the west yard fence!"

Her father kept looking at her. Then he smiled a crooked smile. "But you're a Hunter, and the Hunters don't take any baloney from anybody." He reached over and messed up Maggie's hair. "Look in the mirror! Look at that Hunter beak. Look at those eyeteeth! You're Daddy's girl, honey. You're a fox! A sly fox," he added in a whisper, "who can outsmart anybody—anybody! Including clean-up captains," he said, his eyes glimmering. "And principal's nephews!"

"Dad," said Maggie.

Her father put the newspaper on the table. "Dad, nothing. Let me tell you something," he said. "When I was a freshman at Harvard, a guy on the football team—a linebacker—kept sneaking into the bathroom and putting honey in my shoes every time I took them off to take a shower."

What does Maggie's dad say she should do?

Is Maggie agreeing?

Do you think she will?

What happened to Maggie's dad at college?

Maggie looked at him. "Well, why didn't you lock the bathroom door?"

Her father took a large swallow of juice. "No lock."

"How did you know he was the one who was doing it?"

"The same way you know Corky Newton trashed your lunch. Some things you just know. Anyway, I got tired of having sticky feet. So one time when he went away for the weekend, I borrowed a pig from my cousin in New Hampshire. And I locked it in his dorm room. Of course, a pig has to eat, so I dumped in a couple of trash cans full of rotten food that I found outside the cafeteria."

Maggie smiled.

Her father smiled back.

"Needless to say," he said, "the guy never messed with me again."

How did Maggie's dad get even?

Thinking About What You Read

What did you find out?

1. Why was Mr. Hunter's prank a "just reward"?

_____

_____

_____

2. When Maggie made the comment about finding hair in everything, was she really upset about hair in her bowl and dog hair on her pillow? What was she really upset about?

_____

_____

3. Sometimes, getting even can be hard work. You have to think about all the steps of your plan and what might possibly go wrong with each one. What were the things Mr. Hunter had to think about and plan for when he wanted to get even with the football player? I've written two to start you off.

how to get the pig from New Hampshire

how to keep the pig quiet when he brought it into the dorm

_____

_____

_____

_____

4. What could Maggie do to get even with Corky Newton? What things will she have to think about to carry out her plan? Should she work alone or ask a friend to help her? Write a plan for Maggie. Include some problems she might face and what she should do to solve them.

_____

_____

_____

_____

_____

How did the author help you read the story?

When people try to explain their ideas or their feelings, they often give examples or reasons. Doing this helps their listeners or readers understand what they mean. Mavis Jukes knows this, so her characters give reasons and examples to explain their opinions and feelings.

Think about Maggie's comment, "Everything has hair in it!" Well, just why did Maggie feel so strongly about hair? Ms. Jukes built three examples into her story to explain why Maggie made this statement.

☆ She found a hair in her cereal bowl.

☆ She found dog hair all over her pillow after every weekend visit to her father.

☆ Corky Newton put hair in her sandwich last Friday.

1. Now think about Maggie's problem with Corky Newton. Why did Maggie feel that she couldn't get even with Corky? Reread the story to find the four main reasons she gave. Then write them below. I've written the first one to get you started.

   He's the principal's nephew, and she'll get in trouble if she reports him.

   _____

   _____

   _____

   _____

   _____

   _____

2. Reasons can also help you to convince people of something. They can help you to persuade others to share your opinion. Let's look at one of Mr. Hunter's opinions, for example. He believed that Maggie should *try* to get even with Corky Newton. Maggie, though, thought that the situation was hopeless. What three main reasons did Mr. Hunter give to persuade Maggie to try? I've written two of them below. Add one more to the list.

   She's a Hunter, and the Hunters don't take any baloney from anybody.

   She's Daddy's girl.

   _____

   _____

3. To make his argument even stronger, Mr. Hunter also gave Maggie an example of a way to get even. What was his example?

   _____

   _____

How can you use reasons and examples in your writing to support your opinions and feelings?

Imagine that you're Maggie, and you're going to take your father's advice. But you need someone to help you get even with Corky. Who would you want to help you? What could you say to convince that person to help you? Name your helper below. Then write an argument persuading him or her to help you. Use reasons and examples to support your argument.

Helper: _____

PERSUASIVE ARGUMENT

_____

_____

_____

_____

_____

_____

_____

_____

_____

_____

_____

_____

_____

_____

_____

_____

_____

_____

_____

Getting Ready to Read

1. Look at the snake on this page. What ideas come to mind when you think of snakes? List your ideas below.

_____   _____

_____   _____

2. Are snakes always bad? Can they be good? Think of some reasons why people might consider snakes to be bad or good and list them below. I've started each list for you.

Why Snakes Are Bad   **Why Snakes Are Good**
Some can kill people.   *Some eat rodents and other pests.*

_____   _____

_____   _____

Here's a little bit of background information about the story you're going to read.

Long ago a python named Nyangara was the doctor for a village chief. Whenever the chief felt ill, he would send for Nyangara. The snake would then come to make the chief feel better.

One day, when the chief was very sick, he sent the grown-up men of the village to fetch the python. When the men returned, though, they were empty-handed! They had been so frightened of the great, uncoiling snake that they had run away.

Now the chief had a terrible problem. He was growing weaker and weaker, and he didn't know whom to send for Nyangara. What was the chief to do?

Reading

Read the story that begins on the next page to find out what happens next. Answer the questions in the margin while you read.

NYANGARA, the Python

as told by Hugh Tracey

"Father, let *us* go up the hill to fetch your Doctor."

And the Chief said,

"Thank you . . . my children. I will teach you . . . the magic song . . . which you must sing . . . outside the cave . . . of Nyangara." So he taught them the song, and he said,

"Now . . . my children . . . you must take . . . another pot of beer . . . to my Doctor . . . as a present . . . from me."

Who offered to help the Chief?

What two things must the children do?

So, twenty little children took the pot of beer and set off. Up, up, up they climbed, right up to the top of the hill and they stood in a row outside the cave of the Python and began to sing,

"Please, please, Nyangara-we,
We want to see you Nyangara.

Please, please, Nyangara-we,
Our Chief is dying, Nyangara.

Nyangara come out,
Nyangara come out."

And the Python answered them from within, saying,

"Yes, yes, children of the Chief,
Climb up here.
Others came here only yesterday,
Ha-a-ia, climb up here.

They broke the pot of beer and ran away.
Are *you* going to run away?"

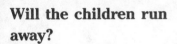

Will the children run away?

But the children stood stock still and went on singing.

"Please, please Nyangara-we,
We want to see you Nyangara."

And then the Python began to uncoil himself and come out of the cave. He uncoiled three . . . four . . . six . . . seven . . . nine, all ten coils, and came right out of his cave. Then he curled himself up onto the shoulders of nineteen little children, and the twentieth walked in front with the pot of beer on his head, out of which the Python drank as they went along.

So they brought him down, down the hill to the Chief's hut. And they put him down outside the door. They opened the door and looked inside, and there was the Chief, lying on his mat, and he was very sick indeed.

Where did the Python ride?

Then the Python went inside the hut and they shut the door after him.

So Nyangara the Python set about the Chief at once. He licked him all over his back, down his legs, up his front, and all over his face; and when he had finished licking his face, the Chief woke up, quite well again, and he said,

"Thank you, my Python, for coming to see me. Now I'll send you back to your home in the cave."

So he called the little children and said,

"Take my Python, my Nyangara, back to his cave on top of the hill, and when you go, take him an ox as a present from me."

So the little children took Nyangara back to his cave. And when they came back, the Chief said,

"Now, my children, you can take another ox for yourselves, and have a feast of meat. But don't you let the grown-ups have any, for *they* would have let me die."

What did the Python do to the Chief?

What was the Python's reward?

How were the children rewarded?

Thinking About What You Read

What did you find out?

1. How did the Chief "reward" the grown-ups? Why was this a just reward?

_____

_____

_____

2. If you were one of the children, how would you have felt when the Python began to uncoil?

_____

_____

_____

3. We know that the Chief gave rewards to the Python and to the children. But how did the Chief decide that they had served him well? What actions might the Chief have considered when thinking about the proper reward for the Python and for the children? List those actions below. I've started both lists for you.

The Children's Service	The Python's Service
went directly to the cave	_worked quickly_
_____	_____
_____	_____

How did the author help you read the story?

The author wanted his readers to understand just how sick the Chief was. He also wanted to tell us that the Chief kept growing weaker. One way he could have done this would have been simply to write, "The Chief was very, very sick. Every day he grew weaker." But that's not a very interesting way of writing, is it? So what did the author do? Let's take a look.

1. Reread the story. Find the two paragraphs where the Chief speaks for the first time. Draw a box around these paragraphs. How did the author signal us that the Chief was ill and weak?

_____

_____

This punctuation tells us to pause. In these two paragraphs, the author wanted to show that speaking was a big effort for the Chief. So he built pauses into the Chief's sentences.

2. Now find another paragraph where the author used the same punctuation marks. Underline the sentence in which they appear. What purpose do those marks serve here?

_____

_____

How can you use a series of three periods in your writing to show effort and the passing of time?

Once the Python returned home, he reported his success to his family. What did he say about how hard and how long he had worked to cure the Chief? Write the Python's story on the lines below. Use the series of three periods to help you show effort and the passing of time.

_____

_____

_____

_____

_____

_____

_____

_____

_____

_____

_____

_____

_____

_____

_____

_____

_____

_____

_____

GOTCHA!

Don't look now, but your face is REALLY RED! You've been caught! Admit it!

Sometimes embarrassing things happen to us. When we are embarrassed, our faces feel hot and may even turn red.

1. What is the most embarrassing thing that ever happened to you?

_____

_____

_____

_____

2. What were your feelings when that happened? On the lines below, write some words that describe how you felt.

_____   _____

_____   _____

3. Have you ever embarrassed anyone else? What did you do?

_____

_____

_____

4. Now let's see just how embarrassed you'd be if any of the things I've listed on the next page ever happened to you. Read about each situation and then use a red pen or pencil to mark your "embarrassment temperature" on the thermometer. Start at the bottom of the thermometer and work your way up. For each situation, color the number of spaces that would show how embarrassed you'd be. Color one space red if you'd feel *some* embarrassment, but not enough so that anybody would notice. Color five blocks red if you'd feel *completely* embarrassed. Just how high will your embarrassment temperature go?

A. You're caught peeking through someone's kitchen window.

B. At lunch you drip mustard on your shirt.

C. Your mother makes you use a table napkin the size of a sheet.

D. You give the wrong answer to a simple riddle.

E. You're racing a bossy older kid on bikes. You really want the older kid to do something foolish and lose the race. But the older kid is a great bike rider and beats you by a mile.

F. You want to show how well you can skate on one foot, but you end up flat on your face.

G. If you're a boy, you lose a contest of skill to a girl. If you're a girl, you lose a contest of skill to a boy.

H. Your tongue gets twisted and you give an incorrect answer. You follow with the right answer, but since the wrong one came out first, your team loses the match.

I. You're in line at a fast food place with some new friends. When it's your turn to order and pay, you realize you left your money at home on the kitchen table.

J. You're caught in a part of town where you're not supposed to go.

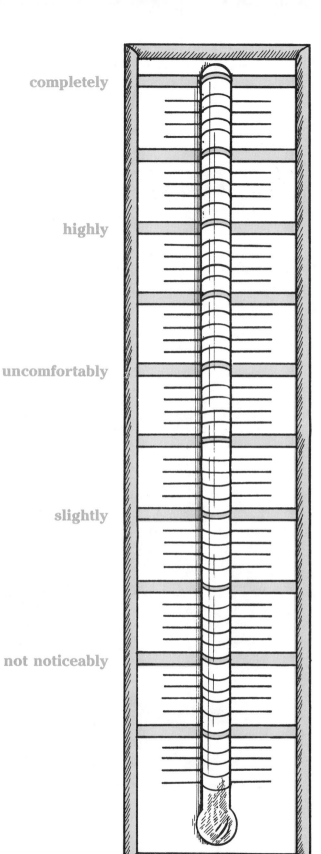

completely

highly

uncomfortably

slightly

not noticeably

EMBARRASSMENT THERMOMETER

Yes, some of those situations really *are* embarrassing, aren't they? Well, some very similar things happen in the stories in this unit. Each one involves a GOTCHA! of some kind. So let's go find out just who or what gets whom!

Getting Ready to Read

Did you see the posters on the corner fence by McLaughlin's store? You didn't? You must have come to school the other way today. Well, here's what you missed!

1. When you go to a carnival, what are some other things you expect to see?

_____   _____

_____   _____

_____   _____

2. Sometimes contests are part of carnivals, too. What contests might you see at a carnival? I've started a list below. Add your ideas to it.

a pie-eating contest

_____   _____

_____   _____

_____   _____

3. Look at the picture above. Name three kinds of contests in which you would use a target like this.

_____

_____

_____

4. Now flip to the next page and quickly read the title of the story. Even if you have never heard of Annie Oakley, you can tell what kind of contest this story will be about. What is it?

_____

_____

5. What might Annie Oakley have to do to win?

_____

_____

Reading

Now read the story that begins on page 80 to see if you guessed right. Answer the questions in the margin while you read.

Who's That Girl with the Gun?
A Story of Annie Oakley

by Robert Quackenbush

What contest was to take place?

Who will win the shooting match?

Who did win?

In 1875, when Annie was fifteen, a marksman named Frank Butler came to Cincinnati with his traveling show. Shows like his were popular back then, in the same way modern sports like baseball, football, basketball, and ice hockey are popular today.

The community was excited because Frank had offered to have a shooting match with the best crack shot in the area. The match would be held in the afternoon. Then people would stay for the evening show "to see some real shooting." Butler was offering a prize of $100.

The big day came and the area's crack shot stepped forward. Frank Butler was flabbergasted to see he was shooting against a girl named Annie Oakley. He was even more flabbergasted when Annie beat him in a close match. Not only that, he fell head over heels in love with her.

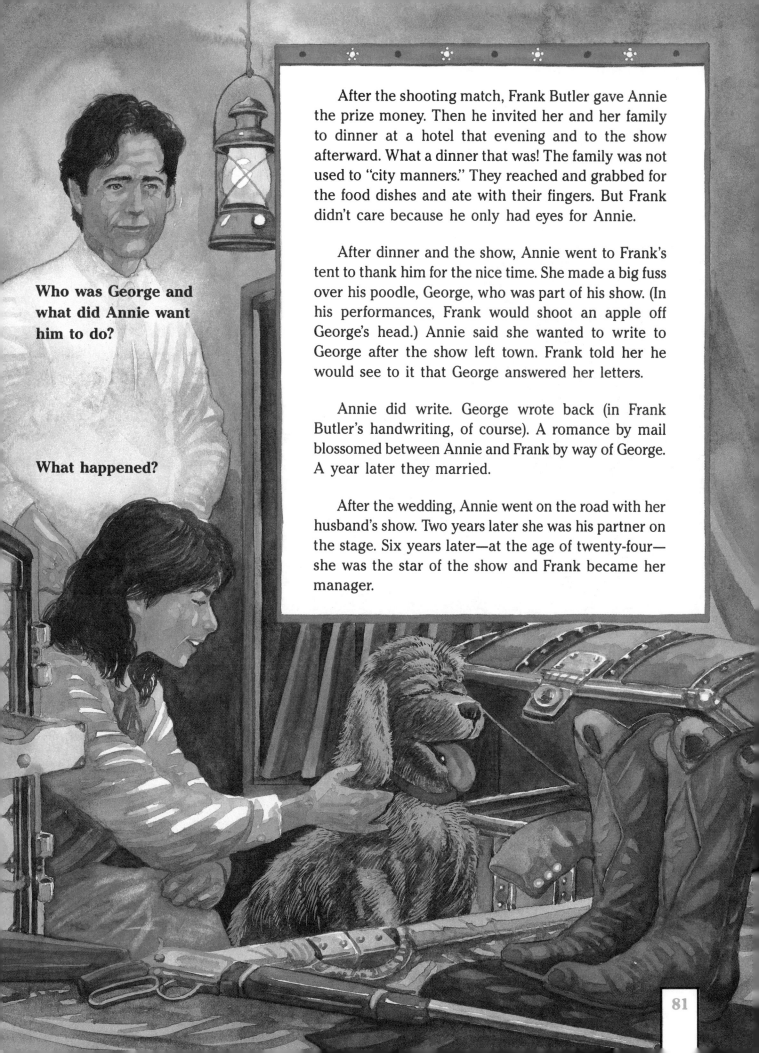

Who was George and what did Annie want him to do?

What happened?

After the shooting match, Frank Butler gave Annie the prize money. Then he invited her and her family to dinner at a hotel that evening and to the show afterward. What a dinner that was! The family was not used to "city manners." They reached and grabbed for the food dishes and ate with their fingers. But Frank didn't care because he only had eyes for Annie.

After dinner and the show, Annie went to Frank's tent to thank him for the nice time. She made a big fuss over his poodle, George, who was part of his show. (In his performances, Frank would shoot an apple off George's head.) Annie said she wanted to write to George after the show left town. Frank told her he would see to it that George answered her letters.

Annie did write. George wrote back (in Frank Butler's handwriting, of course). A romance by mail blossomed between Annie and Frank by way of George. A year later they married.

After the wedding, Annie went on the road with her husband's show. Two years later she was his partner on the stage. Six years later—at the age of twenty-four—she was the star of the show and Frank became her manager.

81

Why did people come to see Annie?

Everywhere they went, Annie attracted huge crowds. People wanted to see the girl who made magic with a rifle. In her Western outfit, Annie would run into the sawdust ring, take a quick bow, and begin. She would shoot the ash from a cigarette that Frank held in his mouth. She would shoot the center spot in a five of spades playing card that Frank held in his hand. She would throw glass balls in the air, turn a cartwheel or leap over a table, grab a rifle, and break the balls before they hit the ground. She would shoot the flames off a turning wheel of candles. What she could do with firearms was nothing short of miraculous. The crowds went wild when they saw a pretty girl, barely five feet tall and weighing less than a hundred pounds, who could shoot better than anyone.

Thinking About What You Read

What did you find out?

1. Complete the timeline below to show the important dates and events in Annie's life. Write what Annie did and how old she was when she did it.

1875   1880   1885

2. What are some words you could use to describe Annie's shooting? I've written one word to start you off. Add a few more to the list.

accurate _____   _____

_____   _____

3. How was watching the shooting match between Annie and Frank like watching a basketball game? How was it different?

_____

_____

_____

_____

4. Why do you think Annie wanted to write to George rather than to Frank?

_____

_____

_____

5. What were two "GOTCHA's" that you found in this story?

_____

_____

How did the author help you read the story?

Before Mr. Quackenbush wrote this story, he had to do a lot of reading and other research. He probably read many books and articles about Annie, her family, and Frank. When Mr. Quackenbush finished his research, he really knew a lot about these people and about the times in which they lived. But he knew, too, that he couldn't expect his readers to know all the facts he knew. So the author added a lot of background information to his story. He included the facts that he thought his readers would need to understand his characters' actions and the times. Let's look at some of the places where Mr. Quackenbush gave us background information.

The first place where the author explains something to readers is in the first paragraph of the story. He knew that most readers today wouldn't know much about traveling shows and how popular they were in 1875. Today that type of entertainment is pretty unusual. So what did Mr. Quackenbush do to help you understand the traveling show?

1. Reread that first paragraph. Find the sentence that tells you how popular traveling shows were in Annie's time. Underline that sentence.

2. Now tell in your own words how the author helped you understand how popular traveling shows were.

_____

_____

_____

3. Reread the fourth paragraph of the story. Find another place where Mr. Quackenbush explains something about the people of that time. Underline the sentences that describe how Annie's family behaved at Frank's dinner.

4. Reread the last paragraph of the story. What is the main idea of this paragraph?

_____

_____

What four facts does the author give you to help you understand this main idea? Draw a box around this group of details.

5. Now it's time to use your imagination. Pretend that you're watching one of Annie Oakley's shows. Make up two more details to describe Annie's skills with a gun. Write them here.

_____

_____

_____

_____

_____

How can you use facts and details to help your readers understand what you have written?

In the 1800s people often saved letters to and from the important people in their lives. Some of these letters wound up in family scrapbooks to be reread years later. Pretend that you're Annie Oakley. Write a letter to George. (Remember, Annie was REALLY writing to Frank.) Then write an answering letter from George (Frank). Include facts and details in each letter so that someone who finds your scrapbook in the future will understand what you've written.

Dear George,

_____

_____

_____

_____

_____

_____

_____

_____

Dear Annie,

_____

_____

_____

_____

_____

_____

_____

_____

Let a friend read the letters in your scrapbook. Did your facts and details help your friend understand why you were writing to George?

Getting Ready to Read

**YOU ARE INVITED
TO JOIN
THE SPY PATROL.**

Meeting Time: Monday after school
Place: 1919 Cellars Alley

Official badges will be given to
original members only.

JOIN NOW!

1. What would the members of a Spy Patrol do? Why?

_____

_____

_____

2. What skills would you need to be a spy? List some of them here.

*walk quietly*_____   _____

_____   _____

_____   _____

3. What pieces of equipment does a spy need? List some of them here.

_____   _____

_____   _____

_____   _____

4. Since you know so much about spying, you may become a member of the Spy Patrol. But first you have to prove that you are worthy. Your first assignment is an easy one: You are to spy on someone in your own house. How would you go about it?

_____

_____

_____

By now you've probably figured out that the next story is about spying. You'll need a few background "clues," though, before you begin to read.

One day, Chris and Frank steal a ride in a wheelchair belonging to Frank's grandmother and Chris discovers what looks like a magic stone at the bottom of the chair. After some more facts are uncovered, Chris decides that there's something VERY suspicious about Frank's grandmother. As the grandmother rides to a small cafe in her wheelchair, Chris follows her. The grandmother is supposed to be attending a meeting of the Fine Thread Association of Needleworkers. But if that were true, why would the grandmother's doctor go into the same cafe? Could the doctor spend his spare time doing needlework? Or could the Fine Thread Association meeting be a "cover" for a very different kind of meeting? Hm-m-m-m?

What do you think Chris wants to discover?

_____

_____

_____

_____

Reading

Now grab a decoder and read the story that begins on page 88. Answer the questions in the margin while you read.

The Magic Stone

by Leonie Kooiker

He had hidden just in time. Apparently all the members of the club hadn't arrived yet. A small man with a black, pointed beard and a head sunk between his shoulders came along, and then two fashionably dressed ladies. He would never have thought they would be involved in witchcraft. As quickly and noiselessly as the others, they vanished through the door that you didn't even notice until you went right up to it, so little did it look like a door.

I wish I could see what they're doing, Chris thought. At the end of the alley, extending from the cafe wall, was a wooden fence, awfully high, but if he climbed on the wheelchair, he might be able to hoist himself to the top and peer over it. Nobody had come along for quite a while, and Chris was tired of skulking there in the alley. By now he had clean forgotten about his trumpet lesson.

He climbed onto the wheelchair seat and pulled himself up. Right against the fence, so close that only a cat could slip through between, was a shed. He managed to get up on its roof and cautiously slid forward until he could see something.

What kind of meeting did Chris think they were having?

What did Chris wish he could do?

Where was Chris supposed to be?

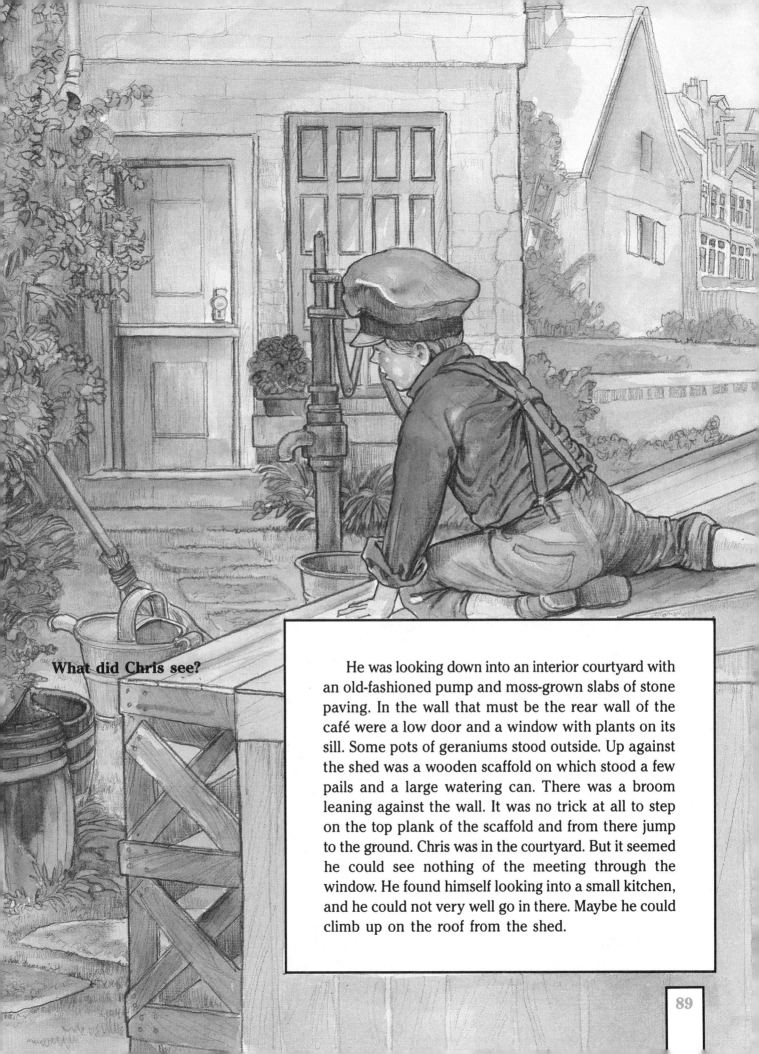

What did Chris see?

He was looking down into an interior courtyard with an old-fashioned pump and moss-grown slabs of stone paving. In the wall that must be the rear wall of the café were a low door and a window with plants on its sill. Some pots of geraniums stood outside. Up against the shed was a wooden scaffold on which stood a few pails and a large watering can. There was a broom leaning against the wall. It was no trick at all to step on the top plank of the scaffold and from there jump to the ground. Chris was in the courtyard. But it seemed he could see nothing of the meeting through the window. He found himself looking into a small kitchen, and he could not very well go in there. Maybe he could climb up on the roof from the shed.

What do you think will happen next?

What happened?

Chris stood quietly looking the shed over. His back was to the little door. A pity that the scaffold isn't closer to the café wall, he thought. The shed roof didn't look any too solid.

"What are you doing here?"

With a start, he turned around. He had heard nothing, but suddenly two people stood there, the red-haired young woman and the doctor. They fixed penetrating stares upon him. The woman had green eyes, and the doctor's eyes had a sinister glitter under those bushy eyebrows. Chris had to think fast.

Thinking About What You Read

What did you find out?

1. What might have brought the red-haired woman and the doctor out to the courtyard? Write two possibilities below.

_____

_____

2. Chris has a big problem now. He has to answer the question, "What are you doing here?" What are two excuses he might come up with for being in the courtyard? What reason could he give for each excuse?

Excuses   Reasons

A. _____   A. _____

   _____   _____

B. _____   B. _____

   _____   _____

3. In what order did Chris take the following actions? Number them from *1* to *5*.

_____ He got up on the roof of the shed.   _____ He jumped into the courtyard.

_____ He climbed onto the wheelchair.   _____ He slid forward on the roof.

_____ He stepped on the top plank of the scaffold.

4. Chris had to take certain steps in order to carry out his spying task. Think of a time when you had to do something that involved a number of steps. (If you were spying on someone, you might have had to get a closer look. Or you might have had to get a ball from a neighbor's yard, or rescue a cat or a kite from a roof or a tree.) What steps did you have to take to carry out your task? In what order did you take them? Write the steps, in order, on the lines below.

_____

_____

_____

_____

_____

How did the author help you read the story?

You know that when you're spying on someone, you have to notice a lot of tiny details. Each one might become very important. Ms. Kooiker knew this, too. She wrote this part of her story very carefully, so that you could be there with Chris as he peered into the courtyard. Ms. Kooiker used as many **descriptive words** as she could to help you see what Chris saw.

1. What DID Chris see when he looked down from the roof? Without rereading the story, list the things you remember that were in the courtyard. Then after you've listed everything you can remember, find the paragraph that describes the courtyard. Add the items you didn't remember to your list.

_____   _____

_____   _____

_____   _____

_____   _____

_____   _____

2. Ms. Kooiker also described the people Chris saw. Reread the story and underline the parts that tell you how the people looked. Could you draw a picture of each of these people and feel you had the right idea? Why?

_____

_____

3. Now think about how the author described *where* things were. Look again at your list from question 1. Then draw each item where you think it should be on the plan below. If necessary, reread the story for clues. I've started the plan for you.

café

courtyard

alley

How can you use descriptive words in your writing?

Follow Chris as the doctor and the red-haired woman take him into the café. What would Chris see there? What would other members of the Fine Thread Association of Needleworkers look like? Where would they be positioned in the café? Write a description of what Chris would see inside the café. Then give your writing to a friend and ask your friend to draw a picture of what you've described. Did you help your friend see everything?

3

Getting Ready to Read

Doesn't EVERYBODY love pizza? Mm-m-m-m. Just the thought of it makes me hungry.

1. What kind of pizza do you like? Write some words to describe your favorite kind in the slices to the right.

2. How could you write those words to make them look interesting to someone else? Here's an idea for one way you could write the word *hot.*

Choose two or three of your own words and write them in an interesting way.

3. Now let's SELL that pizza! Make up a really catchy saying to use in an ad for your pizza. Make it so mouth-watering that EVERYONE will want some of your pizza!

_____

4. Wait a minute! We're still in a unit called GOTCHA! How does pizza fit in?

_____

_____

Reading

Now that your mouth is watering, read the poem on page 95.

The Hot Pizza Serenade

(Sung to the tune of "There's a Small Hotel")

by Frank Jacobs

There's a strange new dye
On my fav-rite tie—
I got it when I ate
Hot Pizza!

There's a glob of glue
On my new suede shoe—
I got it when I ate
Hot Pizza!

Each time that I eat it
I am dropping Mozzarella!
I need an umbrella—
Sloppy fella!

When my clothes have spots
Thick as Polka dots,
I scrape the greasy stuff
From my collar, shirt and cuff,
And I know I've had enough
Hot Pizza!

Thinking About What You Read

1. Why is this poem included in this unit?

_____

_____

2. Just *why* do people get pizza all over their clothes? List a few reasons below.

_____

_____

_____

3. The poet thought an umbrella might solve his problem. What other things could he do to solve the problem? Write your ideas below.

_____

_____

_____

4. Is eating pizza worth taking the chance of getting stains on your clothes? Why or why not?

_____

_____

_____

5. What other foods can you think of that are like pizza? How are they similar to pizza?

Food	Similarities
_____	_____
_____	_____
_____	_____

6. Do you think the poet LIKES pizza? What makes you think that?

_____

_____

_____

How did the poet help you read the poem?

Frank Jacobs wrote this poem to entertain you. He wanted you to enjoy reading about his experiences with pizza.

1. What kinds of things can be expressed better in a poem than in other types of writing?

_____

_____

_____

Mr. Jacobs helped you read his poem by giving you important information before you read his words. He told you that the poem is to be sung to a particular musical melody. So even if you don't know the tune, you do know that the rhythm of this poem is special.

2. Mr. Jacobs also used some marks of punctuation to help you understand the rhythm of his poem. Reread the poem and underline the lines that have special punctuation. What is that mark of punctuation called?

_____

You probably underlined the three lines that have **dashes** at the end, didn't you? Well, you're right! These dashes serve an important purpose: They tell readers to hold the final sound of the word just a little longer, so that this line will work with the sound of the line above it.

3. Try saying the poem quietly to yourself now. How do you say the first two lines of the first verse? How do you say the second two lines?

_____

_____

_____

How do the dashes help you do this?

_____

_____

_____

How can you use familiar tunes and dashes to help you write a poem?

There's an old song that lots of people know. It's called "On Top of Old Smokey." Do you know it?

I remember a funny poem from when I was your age. It was sung to the tune of "On Top of Old Smokey." Maybe you still sing it.

On top of spaghetti
All covered with cheese—
I lost my poor meatball
When somebody sneezed.

Now choose a tune you know and write your own food poem to it. Use dashes when you want your readers to hold the sounds of words or to pause. Write as many verses as you can.

4

Getting Ready to Read

That octopus is really something, isn't it? If I had to play all those instruments at once, I know I'd be "tentacle-tied"! What about you?

1. What are some activities you wish you could do REALLY well? List them here. (To start the list, I wrote one thing *I'd* like to do really well!)

tap-dance

_____   _____

_____   _____

_____   _____

2. Now think about any three of the activities you listed above. What special skills does each one require? Add your three activities, and the skills you need for them, to this chart.

Activity	Skills Required
tap dancing	*rhythm* *balance* *grace*

3. Most likely, the skills for your activities repeated at least one of the skills needed to tap-dance well. If swimming isn't one of the activities you listed, which of the skills on your chart would you need to swim well? If you think you need any other skills to swim well, write them on this list.

_____   _____

_____   _____

_____   _____

4. The title of the next story is *The Night Swimmers*. What GOTCHA! is likely to happen in a story with that title?

_____

_____

_____

Reading

Now read the story that begins on page 101. Be on the lookout for the GOTCHA! as you read. It might be very different from the one you expect! Answer the questions in the margin while you read.

The Night Swimmers

by Betsy Byars

When the swimming pool lights were turned out and Colonel and Mrs. Roberts had gone to bed, the Anderson kids came out of the bushes in their underwear. They moved silently over the moss-smooth lawn, across the Moroccan tiled terrace.

At the edge of the pool they stopped. Retta, the girl, said, "See, I told you it was beautiful." She stared at the shimmering water as proudly as if she had made the pool instead of just discovered it one day.

"But what if somebody sees us?" Roy asked. He hiked up his underwear uneasily. The elastic was sprung, and he wasn't sure the safety pin was going to hold.

"No one's going to see us. It's too dark." She shrugged as if it didn't matter anyway. "The shallow end's down here. Come on."

She led them to the end of the pool, and together the three of them started down the steps.

"It's cold," Roy said. He clutched his underwear tighter, pulling it toward his chest.

"You'll get used to it."

Abruptly Johnny pulled away. "I want to go down the ladder," he said. He started around the pool.

Retta frowned slightly. Lately Johnny had started doing things his own way. "All right," she called after him, belatedly giving permission, "but then you swim right over to the shallow end, you hear me? I don't want to have to come in and save you."

"You won't." As Johnny took hold of the smooth metal ladder, an adult feeling came over him. He entered the water slowly—it was cold—and then pushed off. He dog-paddled to Retta and Roy, turning his head from side to side in a motion he thought made his dog paddle look more powerful.

"Now you two play here in the shallow end while I do some swimming," Retta said when Johnny joined them.

What was Roy afraid might happen?

What doesn't Retta want to have to do?

"I don't see why I have to stay in the shallow end," Johnny said.

"Because only one can go in the deep water at a time. That's a rule, and you already had your turn."

What was Roy doing?

Beside them Roy was pretending to swim. He had one hand on the bottom of the pool and was lifting the other arm in an elaborate swimming stroke. Then he put that hand on the bottom and lifted the other. "Want to see me swim, Retta?"

Why was Johnny watching Retta?

"That's nice, Roy," she said. She moved toward the deep end and began to swim silently. She was aware that Johnny was watching her, hoping to find fault, so she moved with deliberate grace. She copied the movements she had seen the Aquamaids do on television. She turned on her back. Then she swirled and dived under the water. Her bare feet rose, toes pointed, and shone in the moonlight.

Thinking About What You Read

1. What was the GOTCHA! in this story?

_____

_____

_____

2. *Why* was Johnny hoping to find fault with Retta's swimming?

_____

_____

3. Tell about a time you did something perfectly while someone else watched, hoping you'd do it wrong.

_____

_____

4. How did you feel when you "got" that person? Write some words to describe your feelings.

_____   _____   _____

How do you think the other person felt? Write a few words to describe that person's feelings.

_____   _____   _____

5. On the other hand, have you ever ended up looking foolish when you tried to do something perfectly? What were you trying to do? Why did you end up looking silly?

_____

_____

_____

6. As Retta and the boys are swimming, she states the rule that "only one can go in the deep water at a time." Is this a good rule? Why?

_____

_____

_____

7. What are three other rules for swimming safely that you would make if you were Retta?

_____

_____

_____

How did the author help you read the story?

When Ms. Byars wrote this part of her story, she wanted her readers to know exactly *how* certain actions were being taken. She wanted to give us a real "feel" for the way the Anderson children were doing things. To do this, the author used **adverbs.** Adverbs are words that are often used to tell *how* actions are completed. Many adverbs end in *-ly.* Let's think about some of these *-ly* adverbs.

1. It's pretty hard to sneak into someone's pool at night and not be heard, isn't it? What *-ly* adverbs do you know that would tell *how* you'd have to move so that you wouldn't be heard? I've written one in the swimming pool on the right. Add four of your own.

noiselessly

2. Now reread the story to find the *-ly* adverb that Ms. Byars used to tell you exactly *how* each action listed below was done. Write each adverb on the right.

A. The Anderson kids moved over the moss-smooth lawn.

_____

B. Retta stared at the shimmering water.

_____

C. Roy hiked up his underwear.

_____

D. Johnny pulled away.

_____

3. Let's see if you can do a bit of story-writing yourself. Read the author's sentences below. I've underlined the *-ly* adverb the author used in each one. On the line next to each sentence, write an *-ly* word that might be used instead of the one the author used.

A. He entered the water <u>slowly</u>—it was cold—and then pushed off.

_____

B. She moved toward the deep end and began to swim <u>silently</u>.

_____

How can you use -ly *adverbs in your writing to tell how actions were done?*

Ah, there goes Retta underwater. Her body sinks as the water closes over her disappearing feet. How will Retta move when she gets below the water? How will she come up from her underwater swim?

Make a list of some *-ly* adverbs that you might want to use to describe Retta's swimming. I've started your list for you.

powerfully

_____   _____

_____   _____

_____   _____

Now write a paragraph or two about Retta's underwater swim. Include the *-ly* adverbs from your list, plus any others you can think of. When you are finished, share your description with a friend. Compare the *-ly* adverbs you used.

_____

_____

_____

_____

_____

_____

_____

_____

_____

_____

_____

_____

_____

_____

_____

_____

_____

Getting Ready to Read

Just what *is* a riddle? Well, that's a puzzling question! Oh, no...I mean, a *riddle* is a puzzling question. To answer riddles, we sometimes have to look at what we know in a new way.

1. Read the riddle below. Then write your answer to it.

> It's not my sister.
> It's not my brother.
> But it is a child
>   of my father and mother.

Who is it? _____

There are many different kinds of riddles. Some really make you think hard to find the answer. Sometimes riddles even take the form of arithmetic problems! But many riddles are just for fun, even though you still have to find the right answer to the puzzle.

2. Let's see if you can come up with the right answer to these comic riddles.

A. Why did the giant throw his watch out the window?

_____

B. What goes up when rain comes down?

_____

C. What do you call a 300-pound gorilla?

_____

Reading

Read the story that begins on page 108. As you might suspect, it is about a riddle. But why does the answer change? Answer the questions in the margin while you read.

LOGIC

by Carol Kendall and Yao-wen Li

Long ago, in a village far removed from Ch'ang An, which was then the capital of China, an old man asked a little boy a teasing question: "Which is closer, Ch'ang An or the sun?"

What is the riddle?

"The sun, of course," said the boy without hesitation.

What is the boy's answer?

"Wellawell," said the old man, smiling. "And why do you say the sun?"

"That's easy," said the boy. "We can see the sun from here, but we can't see Ch'ang An."

The old man thought the boy exceedingly clever, and the next day took him along to the market place to show him off. Throngs of people from the capital passed through this small village, for it was on a main road. The old man and the boy stood under a tree, and the old man pointed out this one and that one from afar, while the boy stared with open mouth at their strange and beautiful clothing.

Why did the old man take the boy to the market place?

108

Now what's the boy's answer?

Why did the boy change his answer?

"Now then," said the old man, when he saw that a goodly crowd had gathered round them under the tree, "tell us, young lad, which is closer: Ch'ang An or the sun?"

Promptly the boy answered, "Ch'ang An, of course."

The old man's mouth sagged in disappointment. "But—but—only yesterday you told me the sun was closer."

"Yes," said the boy, "but that was before we saw all these people from Ch'ang An. Have you ever seen anyone who came from the sun?"

Thinking About What You Read

What did you find out?

1. Who "got" whom in this story? How did he do it?

_____

_____

_____

2. In what way were the boy's two answers alike? Did they both make sense? Why or why not?

_____

_____

_____

3. Do you think the old man was still disappointed with the boy's answer after he heard the reason for changing it? Why or why not?

_____

_____

_____

4. What is the point of this story?

_____

_____

_____

How did the authors help you read the story?

Ms. Kendall and Ms. Li used very simple language to tell this story. They *didn't* use a lot of descriptive words on purpose because they wanted us to focus on the riddle. But was the point of this story really in the riddle itself—in the question and its answers? Or did we find the point somewhere else? Let's think about that for a minute.

1. Reread the first four paragraphs of the story. Find the riddle question and the boy's answer. Then find the boy's *explanation* of his answer. Write it here.

_____

_____

Isn't the boy's explanation the important part here? Without it, we would never have known just how clever the boy really was. We would never have known the *reason* behind his answer.

2. Now reread the *last* four paragraphs of the story. Find the boy's explanation of his new answer and underline it. Why is this explanation so important?

_____

_____

How can you write great riddles?

Isn't it fun to write riddles that truly stump your friends? The riddle in the story worked because of its explanations. But that's not the only way to make riddles work. Let's look at another way.

This riddle works because it uses a **homophone.** A homophone is a word that *sounds* just like another word, but is often spelled differently and has a different meaning. The homophone in this riddle appears in the question. Can you find the word?

That's right! The homophone is the word *read,* which sounds just like the word *red.* When you <u>hear</u> the question asked, you probably expect the word *red* because of the clue words right before it—*black and white.* But that just leads you into the trick, doesn't it? And that's why this is such a good riddle.

1. This same riddle can have other answers, too, can't it? Pretend that you heard this question asked: "What's black and white and red all over?" What would your answer be? I've written one for you. You write another.

an embarrassed zebra _____   _____

Now let's look at another riddle that also uses homophones. In this riddle, though, the homophone is in the answer rather than in the question.

Question: What do you call a
            perfectly round
            chicken egg?

Answer: A fowl ball.

Just what makes this riddle so clever? Well, isn't there a trick word in the answer? That's right! It's the word *fowl.* The author of this riddle is playing with the homophone pair, *fowl* and *foul. Fowl ball* refers, of course, to the round chicken egg. But it's also a wordplay on the baseball term, *foul ball.*

2. What other homophones can you think of? I've written one pair to start you off. Add some other pairs to the list.

bear/bare

_____   _____

_____   _____

_____

3. Well, it's FINALLY your turn! Write at least three riddles, giving both the question and the answer for each one. In each riddle, use a homophone in either the question or the answer. You can use the homophones you wrote above, or any others you can think of.

_____

_____

_____

_____

_____

_____

_____

_____

_____

_____

_____

_____

_____

Ask a friend your riddles. Did you write some real stumpers?